Be Responsible

WARREN W. WIERSBE

While this book is intended for
the reader's personal enjoyment
and profit, it is also designed for
group study. Study questions are
located at the end of the text.

Run So That You May Win
ivictor.com

Victor is an imprint of
Cook Communications Ministries, Colorado Springs, Colorado 80918
Cook Communications, Paris, Ontario
Kingsway Communications, Eastbourne, England

BE RESPONSIBLE
© 2002 by Warren W. Wiersbe

First Printing, 2002
Printed in the United States of America

2 3 4 5 6 7 8 9 10 Printing/Year 05 04 03

Editor: Craig Bubeck
Cover Design: Bill Gray
Cover Photo: Artville
Study Questions: Sue Moroney

Library of Congress Cataloging-in-Publication Data

Wiersbe, Warren W.
  Be responsible / by Warren W. Wiersbe.
    p. cm.
Includes bibliographical references.
  ISBN 1-56476-790-6
  1. Bible. O.T. Kings, 1st--Criticism, interpretation, etc. I. Title.
BS1335.52 .W54 2002
222'.5306--dc21

                                        2001005610

CONTENTS

PREFACE

An ancient proverb says, "A bad workman always blames his tools." William Bennett, a contemporary writer, says, "Responsible persons are mature people who have taken charge of themselves and their conduct, who own their actions and *own up* to them—who *answer* for them."

Finding someone else to blame, denying irresponsibility, and hiding behind lies seem to be the order of the day. A comedian gets laughs when he says, "The devil made me do it." In contrast, President Harry Truman had a sign on his desk that said, "The buck stops here." He wasn't afraid to take responsibility. "If you can't stand the heat," he said, "get out of the kitchen!"

David knew what it meant to be a responsible leader, and so did his son Solomon, until the closing years of his reign. After Solomon's death, the nation divided into the ten tribes of the northern kingdom of Israel and the two tribes of the southern kingdom of Judah. Out of twenty kings who reigned in Judah following Solomon, only eight could be called good kings and responsible men who sought to obey God. For the sake of David, the Lord kept the light shining in Jerusalem and a king on the throne of Judah until the nation was taken captive by Babylon.

But it wasn't only a dozen kings whose irresponsibility brought about the destruction of the city and temple and the captivity of the people. The prophet Jeremiah reminds us that "the sins of her prophets and the iniquities of her priests" also contributed to Israel's downfall (Lam. 4:13, NKJV). Prophets, priests, and kings were God's chosen and anointed leaders for His people, yet during the 450 years of Jewish national history before the fall of Jerusalem, most of the prophets and priests failed both God and the people.

Integrity is one of the vital foundations of society, but integrity involves taking responsibility and facing accountability. This includes leadership in the home and church as well as in the halls of academe and the political chambers. It's one thing to make promises at the church altar or to take an oath of office, but it's quite another to assume responsibility and act with courage and honesty and seek to please

God. As we study 1 Kings, we will see over and over again the importance of moral character in leaders and the tragedy of leaving God out of national affairs.

"Blessed is the nation whose God is the Lord" (Ps. 33:12).

Warren W. Wiersbe

A Suggested Outline of 1 Kings

Theme: Irresponsible leadership destroys nations
Key verses: 1 Kings 9:4-9

I. The kingdom protected (1 Kings 1:1–2:46)

The last days of David (1:1–2:12
The first acts of Solomon (2:13-46

II. The kingdom enriched (1 Kings 3:1–10:29)

God's gift of wisdom (3:1-28)
Organizing the government (4:1-34)
Building the temple (5:1–6:38; 7:13-51)
Dedicating the temple (8:1–9:9)
Building the royal houses (7:1-12)
Miscellaneous royal projects (9:10-24)
Solomon's glory (10:1-29)

III. The kingdom divided (1 Kings 11:1–14:31)

Solomon's folly (11:1-43)
Rehoboam's folly (12:1-24; 14:21-31)
Jeroboam's folly (12:25–14:20)

IV. The kingdoms destroyed (1 Kings 15:1–22:53)

Judah (15:1-24)
Israel (15:25–22:53)

A Suggested Outline of 1 Kings

The two books of Kings record about four hundred years of the history of Israel and Judah, while the two books of Chronicles see the history of the united kingdom and then the kingdom of Judah from the priestly point of view. Besides recording history, these books teach theology, especially the faithfulness of God in keeping His covenant, the sovereignty of God in directing the destinies of all nations, and the holiness of God in opposing idolatry. Especially important is the way all four books magnify the Davidic dynasty and thus prepare the way for the coming of the Messiah. The books of Kings identify eight kings of Judah, descendants of David, who pleased the Lord: Asa (1 Kings 15:9-15); Jehoshaphat (22:41-43); Joash, or Jehoash (2 Kings 12:1-3); Amaziah (14:1-4); Azariah, or Uzziah (15:1-4); Jotham (15:32-38); Hezekiah (18:1-3); and Josiah (22:1-2). The rulers of the Northern Kingdom were not a godly lot and were not part of David's dynasty.

1 KINGS 1:1–2:46
[1 CHRONICLES 29:22-30]

Sunset and Sunrise

"A crisis isn't what makes a person; a crisis shows what a person's made of." In one form or another, you find this statement in the writings of insightful thinkers from antiquity to the present. Another version is, "What life does to you depends on what life finds in you." The same sun that hardens the clay melts the ice.

The kingdom of Israel was facing a crisis because King David was on his deathbed. In facing this crisis, different people responded in different ways.

1. Adonijah the opportunist (1 Kings 1:1-10)
A real leader looks at a crisis and asks, "What can I do that will best help the people?" An opportunist looks at a crisis and asks, "How can I use this situation to promote myself and get what I want?" Opportunists usually show up uninvited, focus attention on themselves and end up making the crisis worse. Adonijah was that kind of person.

The occasion (vv. 1-4). Adonijah was David's oldest living son and was probably thirty-five years old at this time. David's firstborn, Amnon, was killed by Absalom; his second son, Kileab (or Daniel), must have died young because there's no record of his life; and the third son, Absalom, was slain by Joab (1 Chron. 3:1-2). As David's eldest son, Adonijah felt that he deserved the throne. After all, his father was a sick man who would soon die, and it was important that there be a king on the throne of Israel. Like his older brother Absalom (2 Sam. 15:1-6), Adonijah seized his opportunity when David wasn't at his best and was bedfast. However, Adonijah underestimated the stamina and wisdom of the old warrior and ultimately paid for his pride with his life.

Abishag became a companion and nurse for David and was probably officially considered a concubine, so there was nothing immoral about their relationship. She will become a very important person in the drama after David's death (2:13-23). Adonijah made the mistake of thinking that his father was unable to function normally and therefore interfere with his plans, but he was wrong. Instead of being a sympathetic son, Adonijah decided to claim the throne for himself. If he won the support of his siblings, the government leaders, the priests, and the army, he could pull off a coup and become the next king

The traitors (vv. 5-7). Following the example of his infamous brother Absalom (2 Sam. 15:7-12), Adonijah began to promote himself and generate popular support. Like Absalom, he was a handsome man who had been pampered by his father (v. 6; 2 Sam. 13–14), and the unthinking people joined his crusade. Wisely, Adonijah got the support of both the army and the priesthood by enlisting Joab the general and Abiathar the high priest. Both of these men had served David for years and had stood with him during his most difficult trials, but now they were turning against him. Yet Adonijah knew that the Lord had chosen Solomon to be Israel's next king (2:15), and Abiathar and Joab certainly understood this as well. When the Lord gave David His covenant (2 Sam. 7), He indicated that a future son would succeed him and build the temple (1 Chron. 22:8-10), and that son was Solomon (1 Chron. 28:4-7). Adonijah, Abiathar, and Joab were rebelling against the revealed will of God, forgetting that "[t]he counsel of the Lord stands forever" (Ps. 33:11, NKJV).

The faithful (vv. 8-10). Again, like his brother Absalom, Adonijah hosted a great feast (2 Sam. 15:7-12) and invited all his brothers except Solomon (v. 26). He also ignored several other important leaders in the kingdom, including Zadok the high priest, Benaiah the leader of the king's personal guard, Nathan the prophet, and David's "mighty men" (2 Sam. 23).[1] This was a coronation feast and the guests were proclaiming Adonijah as king of Israel (v. 25). Perhaps some of them thought that the ailing King David had actually laid his hands on Adonijah and named him king. After all, Adonijah's brothers were at the feast, which suggested they made no claim to the throne. But surely the guests were aware of the absence of Solomon, Zadok, Benaiah, and Nathan. And did anyone ask when and where Nathan had anointed Adonijah, and if he had been anointed, why the event was so secret? The faithful servants of God and of David had been left out, an obvious clue that Adonijah had named himself as king without any authority from David or the Lord.

Often in Bible history it appears that "truth is fallen in the street, and equity [justice] cannot enter" (Isa. 59:14, NKJV), but the Lord always accomplishes His purposes. "The wicked is snared in the work of his own hands" (Ps. 9:16, NKJV). Adonijah's great feast was the signal David's loyal servants needed to inform David that it was time to name Solomon the next king of Israel.

2. Nathan the loyalist (1 Kings 1:11-53)

If ever King David had a loyal friend and adviser, it was the prophet Nathan. Nathan brought the good news about God's covenant with David and his descendants (2 Sam. 7:1-17), and Nathan also shepherded David through those dark days after the king's adultery with Bathsheba (2 Sam. 12). Nathan must have had musical gifts as well because he helped David organize the worship in the sanctuary (2 Chron. 29:25-26). When Solomon was born, Nathan told the parents that the Lord wanted the boy also named "Jedidiah—beloved of the Lord" (2 Sam. 12:24-25). When Nathan heard about Adonijah's feast and his claim to the throne, he immediately went to work.

Nathan informed Bathsheba (vv. 11-14). Though we haven't read anything about Bathsheba since the birth of Solomon, we must not conclude that she had been unimportant in the affairs of the palace.

Her conduct in this chapter alone is evidence that she was a courageous woman who wanted to do the will of God. To be sure, it was her son who was to be the next king, and if had Adonijah succeeded in gaining the throne, both Bathsheba and her son would be killed (vv. 12, 21). But the fact that Nathan turned immediately to Bathsheba suggests that he knew what the future queen mother could do. Also, the way Adonijah approached her and Solomon received her (2:13-19) indicates that both men recognized her as a woman of influence. It's unfortunate that too many people think of Bathsheba only as "the adulteress" when it was her intervention that saved Israel from disaster at a critical hour.

Bathsheba informed David (vv. 15-21). The prophet had given Bathsheba the words to speak, a brief statement of only two questions that she expanded into a very moving speech. The key word in the dialogue of this entire scenario is "swear," used in verses 13, 17, 29, and 30. Nathan and Bathsheba knew that David had promised that Solomon would be the next king because Solomon was God's choice. David had publicly announced the appointment of Solomon when he announced the building of the temple (1 Chron. 22, 28). When God gave a special name to Solomon, this certainly suggested that he would be David's successor (2 Sam. 12:24-25).

Bathsheba bowed before the king (v. 16, and see 23, 31, 47, 53) and then reminded him of his oath that Solomon would be the next king of Israel. She then informed him that Adonijah was hosting a coronation banquet and that Abiathar and Joab were there with all the royal sons except Solomon. Obviously the banquet was not to honor Solomon! Adonijah had proclaimed himself king, but all Israel was waiting for David's official word concerning his successor. Her *coup de grace* was the obvious fact that if Adonijah became king, he would quickly get rid of both Bathsheba and her son. What David did was a matter of life or death. Abishag was witness to all that Bathsheba said (v. 15).

Nathan informed David (vv. 22-27). While Bathsheba was speaking to her husband, Nathan came into the palace and was announced, so Bathsheba left the room (v. 28) and Nathan entered the bedchamber. He asked the king two questions: Did David announce that

Adonijah would sit on his throne, and had the king done this in secret without telling his servant the prophet (vv. 24, 27). Sandwiched between these two questions was his report that Adonijah was now celebrating his coronation, all the king's sons except Solomon were at the feast, and so were Abiathar and all the military commanders. Nathan didn't mention Joab, but Bathsheba had already done that. What Nathan revealed was that Joab had brought his officers with him, so the army was backing Adonijah. However, David's loyal servants—Nathan, Zadok, and Benaiah—had been ignored. That being the case, Nathan wondered if Adonijah really had the authority to proclaim himself king.

It's very likely that Nathan's recitation of these facts brought to David's memory the terrible days of Absalom's rebellion and he didn't want the nation to experience another civil war. Solomon was a man of peace (1 Chron. 22:9). Reared in the palace, he had no experience of war as did his father; and if there was a civil war, how could he build the temple?

David instructed his loyal servants (vv. 28-37). David responded immediately to the crisis and told Nathan to call Bathsheba back to his bedside. The two were alone (v. 32). David spoke to Bathsheba and reaffirmed the fact that her son Solomon was to be the next king of Israel. He had sworn this to her privately and would not back down on his oath. But then David went even further and *made Solomon his coregent that very day!* "I will surely carry out this day . . ." (v. 30). If David waited too long, Adonijah's rebellion could grow in strength; and after David died, who would have authority to act? By making Solomon his coregent immediately, David stayed in control and Solomon would do his bidding. Solomon was no longer merely prince or even heir apparent: he was now coregent with his father and the king of Israel.

David then asked them to call his loyal servants—Nathan the prophet, Zadok the priest, and Benaiah the head of his personal bodyguard—men he knew he could trust. He instructed them to proclaim Solomon king in a public demonstration at Gihon. This was an important place of springs on the eastern slope of mount Zion less than a mile up the valley (north) from En Rogel where Adonijah was hosting his great feast (v. 9). It wouldn't take long for the news to get to Adonijah! Solomon was to ride David's royal mule, and it was to be announced that Solomon was sharing David's throne as king and would be David's successor. Zadok and Nathan were to anoint Solomon with the holy anointing oil from the tabernacle. The trumpet would be blown, declaring to the people that this was an official event. Solomon was now king and ruler over all Israel and Judah.[2] (See 4:20, 25.)

Benaiah was the son of a priest (1 Chron. 27:5), but he chose a military career and became one of David's mighty men (2 Sam. 23:20-23) and the leader of David's personal guard, the Cherethites and Pelethites (v. 38; 2 Sam. 8:18). After hearing David's instructions, Benaiah spoke up enthusiastically in agreement and thus gave both David and Solomon the support of the soldiers under his command. Later, Solomon would execute Joab for his treachery in following Adonijah and would give his position to Benaiah (2:35). Benaiah was as loyal to Solomon as he had been to David.

The Lord informed Israel (vv. 38-53).[3] Zadok, Nathan, and Benaiah, protected by David's personal troops, obeyed David's instructions to the letter and announced to all Israel that Solomon was king. The people were ecstatic as they played their musical instruments and shouted "God save King Solomon." This shout echoed down the valley and reached En Rogel where the people were shouting "God save King Adonijah" (v. 25).

As they finished their meal, Adonijah and his guests heard the shouting and the sound of the trumpet and wondered what was going on in Jerusalem. Had David died? Was it a declaration of war?

Their questions were answered by the arrival of Jonathan, the son of Abiathar the priest who had assisted David during Absalom's rebellion (2 Sam. 17:17-22). Adonijah thought that Jonathan was bringing good news, but it turned out to be the worst possible news for Adonijah, Abiathar, and Joab. Jonathan's report is that of an eyewitness who saw Solomon riding the king's mule and watched as Zadok and Nathan anointed the new king. But verses 47-48 describe what transpired in David's bedchamber (vv. 36-37), and we wonder where Jonathan obtained this information. Did he hear Benaiah tell his troops that they would now be loyal to Solomon as they had been to David? Did Nathan or Zadok quote David's words to the people?

Jonathan made it clear that Solomon was *at that very moment* the king of Israel. Adonijah, his fellow conspirators, and his guests knew what that meant: they were all under great suspicion. The guests, including the naïve princes, all rose up and fled back to the city for safety, and Adonijah fled to the tabernacle for asylum. This was the tent in Jerusalem, which housed the ark (1 Chron. 16:1, 37). The tabernacle with the other furnishings was at Gibeon (1 Chron. 16:39-40; 1 Kings 3:4). There was an altar there and Adonijah took hold of the horns of the altar, which is what people in danger did before the establishment of the six cities of refuge (2:28; Ex. 21:13-14). A place of asylum at least delayed judgment and gave the accused an opportunity for a hearing (Deut. 19).

Solomon showed mercy to his brother and allowed him to return to his home in Jerusalem. This amounted to house arrest because the king's guards could keep Adonijah under constant surveillance. But Solomon also warned his brother to be careful how he behaved, for as an insurgent, Adonijah was worthy of death.[4] If he stepped out of line, he would be executed. Adonijah bowed before Solomon, but his heart was submitted neither to the Lord nor his brother.

3. David the realist (1 Kings 2:1-11; 1 Chron. 29:26-30)
David "served his own generation by the will of God" (Acts 13:36, NKJV), but he was also concerned about Solomon and the next generation. David had his enemies, some of whom were in his own household and inner circle, and he wanted to be certain that the new king didn't inherit old problems. During his long reign of forty years, David had unified the nation, defeated their enemies, successfully organized kingdom affairs, and made more than adequate preparation for the building of the temple. He sang his last song (2 Sam. 23:1-7) and then gave his last charge to Solomon.[5]

"Put the Lord first" (vv. 1-4). The Old Testament records the last words of Jacob (Gen. 49), Moses (Deut. 33), Joshua (23:1–24:27), and David (1 Kings 2:1-11). "I go the way of all the earth" is a quo-

tation from Joshua at the end of his life (Josh. 23:14), and "Be strong and show yourself a man" sounds like the Lord's words to Joshua at the start of his ministry (Josh. 1:6). Solomon was a young man who had lived a sheltered life, so he needed this admonition. In fact, from the very outset of his reign, he would have to make some tough decisions and issue some difficult orders. David had already commissioned Solomon regarding building the temple (1 Chron. 22:6-13), a task that would take seven years. One day Solomon would come to the end of his life, and David wanted him to be able to look back with satisfaction. Blessed is that person whose heart is right with God, whose conscience is clear and who can look back and say with the Master: "I have glorified You on the earth. I have finished the work which You have given Me to do" (John 17:4, NKJV).

David's words parallel those of Moses when he commissioned Joshua (Deut. 31). First Moses admonished Joshua to "be a man" and face his responsibilities with courage and faith (vv. 1-8), and then Moses gave the law to the priests and admonished the people (including Joshua) to know it and obey it. The king was expected to be familiar with the law and the covenant (Deut. 17:14-20), for in obeying God's Word he would find his wisdom, strength, and blessing.[6]

But David also reminded his son of the special covenant the Lord had made concerning the Davidic dynasty (v. 4; 2 Sam. 7:1-17). He warned Solomon that if he disobeyed God's law, he would bring chastening and sorrow to himself and the land, but if he obeyed God's commandments, God would bless him and the people. More important, God would see to it that there was always a descendant of David sitting on the throne. David knew that Israel had a ministry to perform in providing the vehicle for the promised Redeemer to come to earth, and the future of God's redemptive plan rested with Israel. How tragic that Solomon didn't fully follow God's law and was the means of promoting idolatry in the land and then causing the kingdom to be divided.

"Protect the kingdom!" (vv. 5-9). David knew that there were perils lurking in the shadows in the kingdom and he warned Solomon to act immediately and deal with two dangerous men. *Joab,* commander of David's army, was the first to be named. He had stood by David

through many difficult trials, but from time to time he had asserted his own will and been guilty of murdering innocent men. Joab was David's nephew and the brother of Abishai and Asahel, and all of them were noted warriors. But Joab killed Abner because Abner had killed Asahel (2 Sam. 2:12-32). Joab also killed David's son Absalom even though he knew David wanted him taken alive (2 Sam. 18). He murdered Amasa, whom David had appointed leader of his forces (2 Sam. 20), and he supported Adonijah in his quest for the throne (1 Kings 1:7). Joab had been involved in David's scheme to kill Bathsheba's husband Uriah (2 Sam. 11:14ff), and perhaps the crafty general was using his knowledge to intimidate the king. David didn't mention Uriah or Absalom to Solomon, and Solomon already knew that Joab was a traitor to the king.

The second dangerous man was *Shimei* (*vv. 8-9*). He was a Benjamite and a relative of Saul who wanted to see Saul's line restored to the throne. He cursed David when David was fleeing from Absalom (2 Sam. 16:5-13). To curse the king was a violation of the law (Ex. 22:28), but David accepted this unkindness as a discipline from the Lord. Later, when David returned to the throne, Shimei humbled himself before the king and David forgave him (2 Sam. 19:18-23). But David knew that there was always a pro-Saul element in the northern tribes, so he warned Solomon to keep Shimei under surveillance.

David not only remembered dangerous men like Joab and Shimei, but he also remembered helpful men like *Barzillai* (*v. 7*), who had provided him and his people with what they needed when they fled from Absalom (2 Sam. 17:27-29). David had wanted to reward Barzillai with a place at his table, but the old man preferred to die in his own home. He asked David to give the honor to his son Kimham (2 Sam. 19:31-38); but now David instructed Solomon to care for Barzillai's sons and not Kimham alone.

David did go "the way of all the earth," and "died in a good old age, full of days and riches and honor..." (1 Chron. 29:28, NKJV). Solomon was already king and his throne was secure, so there was no need for any official decisions or ceremonies.

4. Solomon the strategist (1 Kings 2:12-46)

The new king had his agenda all prepared: deal with Joab, deal with Shimei, reward the sons of Barzillai, and build the temple. But his first major crisis came from his half brother Adonijah.

Adonijah's request (vv. 13-25). Solomon had graciously accepted Adonijah's submission to the new regime (1:53), although Solomon certainly knew that the man was deceitful and ready to strike again. The fact that Adonijah went to the queen mother with his request suggests that he expected her to have great influence with her son. Adonijah's declaration in verse 15 shows how confused he was in his thinking, for if Solomon was God's choice for the throne, and Adonijah knew it, why did he attempt a coup and try to seize the crown? Like Absalom, he thought that a popular demonstration and the cheers of the people meant success. Perhaps Adonijah said "it was his [Solomon's] from the Lord" just to impress Bathsheba.

Students differ in their interpretation of Bathsheba's role in this scenario. Some say she was very naïve in even asking Solomon, but Bathsheba had already proved herself to be a courageous and influential woman. It's likely that she suspected another plot because she knew that possession of a king's wife or concubine was evidence of possession of the kingdom. This was why Absalom had publicly taken David's concubines (2 Sam. 16:20-23), for it was an announcement to the people that he was now king. It's difficult to believe that the king's mother was ignorant of this fact. I may be in error, but I feel that she took Adonijah at his word, *knowing that Solomon would use this as an opportunity to expose Adonijah's scheme.* By having Abishag as his wife, Adonijah was claiming to be coregent with Solomon!

Solomon immediately detected the reason behind the request and said, "Ask for him the kingdom also!" The king knew that Adonijah, Abiathar, and Joab were still united in gaining control of the kingdom. By asking for Abishag, Adonijah issued his own death warrant, and Benaiah went and took the traitor's life. David wasn't there to feel the pain of another son's death, but the execution of Adonijah was the final payment of the fourfold debt David had incurred (2 Sam. 12:5-6). The baby died, Absalom killed Amnon, Joab killed Absalom, and Benaiah executed Adonijah. David paid for his sins fourfold.

Abiathar's removal (vv. 26-27). But Solomon didn't stop there: he also defrocked Abiathar the priest, who had supported Adonijah, and sent him into retirement at the priestly city of Anathoth, about three miles from Jerusalem. This had been the home of Jeremiah the prophet. In deposing Abiathar, Solomon fulfilled the prophecy given to Eli that his family would not continue in the priesthood (1 Sam. 2:27-36; see Ezek. 44:15-16). Zadok was made high priest (v. 35), and his descendants filled the office until 171 B.C. Solomon recognized the fact that Abiathar had faithfully served his father David, so he didn't have him executed.

Joab's execution (vv. 28-35). Joab no doubt had an efficient spy system, and when he heard the news that Adonijah had been slain, he knew he was next on the list. He fled to the tabernacle David had erected in Jerusalem for the ark of the covenant (2 Sam. 6:17) and there claimed asylum by taking hold of horns of the altar. However, only people who were guilty of manslaughter could do this and claim the right to a trial, and Joab was guilty of both murder and disloyalty to King David and King Solomon. Joab defied both Benaiah and Solomon by refusing to come out of the sacred enclosure, but Solomon was not to be treated in such an arrogant manner by a man who was obviously a traitor and a murderer. Though he was a soldier, Benaiah belonged to a priestly family, so it was legal for him to enter the sacred precincts, and he went and killed Joab at the altar and then buried him. Solomon then promoted Benaiah to be the commander of the army in the place of Joab (v. 35).

It's important to understand that Solomon wasn't simply acting in revenge in the place of his father David. Solomon explained that the death of Joab took away the stain of the innocent blood that Joab had shed when he killed Abner and Amasa. The shedding of innocent blood polluted the land (Num. 35:30-34) and the victim's blood cried out to God for vengeance (Gen. 4:10). The cities of refuge were provided for people who had accidentally killed somebody. They could flee to one of the six cities and be protected until the elders had investigated the case. But murderers like Joab were not to be given any mercy but were to be executed so that the innocent blood they had shed would pollute the land no more (Deut. 19:1-13; 21:1-9; Lev.

18:24-30). Saul's treatment of the Gibeonites had polluted the land and created trouble for David (2 Sam. 21:1-14), and Solomon didn't want that to happen during his reign.

Shimei's daring (vv. 36-46). Since Shimei was related to Saul (2 Sam. 16:5; 1 Sam. 10:21), he was a potential troublemaker who might arouse the tribe of Benjamin against the new king, and perhaps even stir up the ten northern tribes of Israel. David had brought unity and peace the nation and Solomon didn't want Shimei creating problems. He ordered him to move to Jerusalem, build himself a house, and stay in the city. If he left the city and crossed the Kidron Valley, he would die. Jerusalem wasn't that large a city at that time, so Solomon's men could keep their eyes on the Benjamite who had cursed David and thrown dirt and stones at him.

Shimei obeyed for three years and then disobeyed. When two of his slaves ran away and went twenty-five miles to Gath, Shimei decided to go personally and bring them back. Surely he could have hired somebody else to go get the slaves, but he went himself. Perhaps he thought he had fulfilled the terms of the agreement, or maybe he thought the guards weren't watching him. Most likely he was deliberately defying Solomon and pushing the limits just to see what he would do. He found out. Solomon knew that Shimei had left Jerusalem, and when he returned, the king confronted him with his crime. Solomon delivered a brief but powerful speech that condemned him for what he did to David and what he had just done to Solomon, and it ended with Benaiah executing Shimei the traitor.

Solomon was to be a "man of peace" (1 Chron. 22:6-10), and yet he began his reign by ordering three executions. But true peace must be based on righteousness, not on sentiment. "But the wisdom that is from above is first pure, then peaceable . . ." (James 3:17, NKJV). The land was polluted by the innocent blood that Joab had shed, and the land could be cleansed only by the execution of the murderer. David didn't execute Joab, even after Joab killed Absalom, because David knew that he himself had blood on his hands (Ps. 51:14). David was guilty of asking Joab to shed Uriah's innocent blood, but Solomon's hands were clean. Solomon was indeed a "man of peace," and he achieved that peace by bringing about righteousness in the land.

From the human viewpoint, it was sunset for David and sunrise for his son Solomon, but not from the divine viewpoint. "But the path of the just is like the shining sun, that shines ever brighter unto the perfect day" (Prov. 4:18, NKJV). As a leader, David was "as the light of the morning . . . even a morning without clouds" (2 Sam. 23:4, KJV), and for the sake of David, the Lord kept the lamp burning in Jerusalem (1 Kings 11:36; 2 Kings 8:19). Even today, when we read and sing his psalms and study his life, that light shines on us and helps to direct our way.

1 KINGS 3–4
[2 CHRONICLES 1]

Wisdom from Above

When Solomon ascended the throne, the people of Israel soon learned that he was not another David. He was a scholar, not a soldier, a man more interested in erecting buildings than fighting battles. David enjoyed the simple life of a shepherd, but Solomon chose to live in luxury. Both David and Solomon wrote songs, but Solomon is better known for his proverbs. We have many of David's songs in the Book of Psalms, but except for Psalms 72 and 127, and the Song of Solomon, we have none of Solomon's three thousand songs.

David was a shepherd who loved and served God's flock, while Solomon became a celebrity who used the people to help support his extravagant lifestyle. When David died, the people mourned; after Solomon died, the people begged his successor King Rehoboam to lighten the heavy yoke his father had put on their necks. David was a warrior who put his trust in God; Solomon was a politician who put his trust in authority, treaties, and achievement. "King Solomon was among the wisest fools who ever wore a crown," wrote Frederick Buechner.[1]

Solomon is mentioned nearly three hundred times in the Old Testament and a dozen times in the New Testament. He's listed in the genealogy of Jesus Christ (Matt. 1:6-7) and is cited as an example of splendor (Matt. 6:29; Luke 12:27) and wisdom (Matt. 12:42; Luke 11:31). He is identified as the builder of the temple (Acts 7:47). One of the colonnades in the temple was named after him (John 10:23; Acts 3:11; 5:12). His father David was recognized as the ideal leader, and his record became the standard by which every succeeding king of Judah was measured. However, nobody pointed to Solomon as a good example of a godly ruler.

Chapters 3 and 4 describe events that occurred during the first three years of Solomon's reign, before he began to build the temple (6:1), and they describe Solomon in several roles.

1. The peacemaker (1 Kings 3:1a)

Solomon's name comes from the Hebrew word *shalom* which means "peace," and during his reign, the kingdom was at peace with its neighbors. His father David had risked his life on the battlefield to defeat enemy nations and claim their lands for Israel, but Solomon took a different approach to international diplomacy. He made treaties with other rulers by marrying their daughters, which helps to explain why he had seven hundred wives who were princesses, as well as three hundred concubines (11:3). It appears that Solomon entered into treaty arrangements with every petty ruler who had a marriageable daughter! Yet Moses in the law warned the Jewish kings not to multiply wives (Deut. 17:14-20).

His first bride after he became king was the daughter of the pharaoh of Egypt, Israel's old enemy. This alliance indicates that Egypt had slipped much lower on the international scene and that Israel was now much higher, because Egyptian rulers didn't give their daughters in marriage to the rulers of other nations.[2] It's significant that Solomon didn't put his Egyptian wife[3] into the royal palace where David had lived, because it was near the ark of the covenant (2 Chron. 8:11), but housed her in another place until her own palace was completed. He spent seven years building the temple of God but thirteen years building his own palace (1 Kings 6:37–7:1).

Solomon's complex system of treaties cut at the very heart of Israel's unique position as the people of God among the nations of the world. They were God's holy people, a chosen people among whom the Lord himself dwelt (Ex. 33:16; Deut. 4:7-8, 32-34). God had made no covenants with the Gentile nations, nor had He given them His Word, His sanctuary, or His holy priesthood (Rom. 9:1-5). God said to the Jews, "I am the Lord your God, who have separated you from other people" (Lev. 20:24, 26, KJV). As long as Israel trusted the Lord and obeyed Him, the nation would "dwell safely alone" (Deut. 33:28). The prophet Balaam described Israel as "a people dwelling alone, not reckoning itself among the nations" (Num. 23:9, NKJV).

The Lord placed Israel among the Gentile nations to be a witness to them of the true and living God, a "light among the Gentiles" (Isa. 42:6). If Israel had continued to be faithful to the terms of God's covenant (Deut. 27–30), the Lord would have blessed them and used them as an "object lesson" to the pagan nations around them. Instead, Israel imitated the Gentiles, worshiped their idols, and abandoned their witness to the true God. For that reason, God had to chasten them and then send them into captivity in Babylon. God wanted Israel to be the "head" of the nations, but because of her compromise, she became the "tail" (Deut. 28:13, 44). Solomon may have thought he was making political progress by bringing Israel into the family of nations, but the consequence was really spiritual regress. Solomon also entered into lucrative trade agreements with other nations (10:1-15, 22), and the nation prospered; but the price he paid was too high.

The kingdom of Israel prospered only as she trusted God and obeyed the terms of His covenant. If they were true to the Lord, He promised to give them all they needed, to protect them from their enemies, and to bless their labors. But from the very beginning of the Jewish monarchy, Israel's leaders made it clear that they wanted to be "like the other nations" (1 Sam. 8), and Solomon led them closer to that goal. Ultimately, Solomon married many pagan wives and began to worship their false gods, and the Lord had to chasten him. See 1 Kings 11.

2. The builder (1 Kings 3:1b)

Solomon is remembered as the king during whose reign the temple was built (chaps. 5–7; 2 Chron. 2–4). His alliance with Hiram, king of Tyre, gave him access to fine timber and skilled workmen. But he also built his own palace (7:1-12), which seems to have consisted of living quarters plus "the house of the forest of Lebanon," where arms were stored and displayed (10:16-17, KJV), the Hall of pillars, and the Hall of Judgment. He also built a house in Jerusalem for his Egyptian princess wife (2 Chron. 8:11). Official state visitors were overwhelmed by the splendor of these structures (chap. 10).

Though he wasn't a warrior himself, Solomon was concerned about the security of the land. He expanded and strengthened the "Millo" (9:24; 11:27), a protective wall or embankment that David had begun to build (2 Sam. 5:9). The word "millo" means "filling." Solomon had a special interest in horses and chariots and built stables in special "chariot cities" (4:26; 9:17-19; 10:26-29). He became quite a "horse dealer" himself and imported horses and chariots and sold them to other nations (2 Chron. 1:14-17; 9:25-28), no doubt making a good profit on the sales. He also built "store cities" in strategic places (9:15-19; 2 Chron. 8:1-6). At that time, Israel controlled several important trade routes that needed to be protected, and military personnel were housed in these cities, along with supplies of food and arms.

Solomon violated the Law of Moses not only by marrying many wives but also by multiplying horses and depending on chariots (Deut. 17:14-17). Contrary to God's command, Solomon went back to Egypt for both! The king was required to copy out for himself the Book of Deuteronomy (Deut. 17:18-20), and we wonder how Solomon responded when he read the command about wives and horses. Or did he ever meditate on what his father wrote in Psalm 20:7 (and see also 33:16-19)? During Solomon's reign, the outward splendor and wealth of Israel only masked an inward decay that led eventually to division and then destruction.

3. The worshiper (1 Kings 3:2-15)
Solomon certainly made a good beginning, for he "loved the Lord, walking in the statutes of David his father" (v. 3, KJV); but a good beginning doesn't guarantee a good ending. Saul, the first king of Israel, started out with humility and victory, but he ended up being rejected by the Lord and committing suicide on the battlefield. Solomon himself would write in Ecclesiastes 7:8, "The end of a thing is better than its beginning" (NKJV) and "A good name is better than precious ointment, and the day of death than the day of one's birth" (7:1, NKJV). We receive our name soon after birth, and between birth and death, we either enhance that name or debase it. After death, we can't change a bad name into a good name or a good name into a bad name. "Great is the art of beginning," wrote the American poet Longfellow, "but greater the art is of ending."

Consecration (vv. 2-4). God purposed that the people of Israel have a central place of worship and not imitate the nations in Canaan by building "high places"[4] wherever they chose. When Israel entered the land, they were instructed to destroy these "high places" and the idols that were worshiped there (Num. 33:52; Deut. 7:5; 12:1ff; 33:29). However, until the temple was built and centralized worship was established in the land, the people of Israel worshiped the Lord in the "high places." In time, the phrase "high place" began to be used to mean "a place of worship" and the Jews worshiped Jehovah at these temporary shrines.

Gibeon was such a sacred place, for the tabernacle was located there. As a first step toward the construction of the tabernacle, David had moved the ark of the covenant to Jerusalem, but the rest of the tabernacle, including the altar of sacrifice, was still at Gibeon, located five miles north of Jerusalem. Solomon assembled the leaders of Israel and arranged for them to go to Gibeon with him and worship the Lord (2 Chron. 1:1-6). This event would not only be an act of consecration but it would manifest to the people the unity of the nation's leaders. Solomon offered a thousand burnt offerings to the Lord as he and his officers together praised the Lord and sought His face. The burnt offering pictured total dedication to the Lord.

Revelation (v. 5). The assembly lasted all day and the people remained at Gibeon for the night, including King Solomon who was given a remarkable dream from the Lord. David had both Nathan and Gad as his counselors, but there seems to have been no prophet in Solomon's circle of advisers. Twice the Lord spoke to the king through dreams (see 9:1-9). The Lord sometimes communicated His messages through dreams not only to His own servants but also to those of other nations, such as Abimelech (Gen. 20), the Egyptian servants of Pharaoh (Gen. 40), and Pharaoh himself (Gen. 41).

Solomon heard the Lord say, "Ask! What shall I give you?" (v. 5, NKJV). The Lord's command and question were a revelation of God's grace as well as a test of Solomon's heart. (The word "ask" is found eight times in this passage.) What people ask for usually reveals what they really desire, and what they desire depends on how they envision their life's calling. Had Solomon been a warrior, he might have asked for victory over his enemies; but he saw himself as a youthful leader who desperately needed wisdom so he could adequately serve God's chosen people. He had succeeded David, Israel's greatest king, and Solomon knew that the people couldn't help but compare and contrast father and son. But even more, he had been called to build the temple of the Lord, an awesome task for such an inexperienced leader. Solomon knew he couldn't accomplish that great venture without wisdom from heaven.

Petition (vv. 6-9). Solomon's prayer was brief and to the point, and it was spoken with true humility, for three times he called himself "your servant." First, Solomon reviewed the past and thanked God for the faithfulness and steadfast love shown to his father (v. 6). Solomon acknowledged God's goodness in keeping his father through many trials and then giving him a son to inherit his throne. Solomon is referring here to the covenant God gave to David when he expressed his heart's desire to build a temple for God (2 Sam. 7). In that covenant, God promised David a son who would build the temple, and Solomon was that son. Solomon admitted that he wasn't the king because God recognized his abilities but because He kept His promises to his father David.

Then, Solomon moved into the present and acknowledged God's grace in making him king (v. 7). But he also confessed his youthfulness and inexperience and therefore his desperate need for God's help if he was to succeed as Israel's king. Solomon was probably twenty years old at this time and certainly much younger than his advisers and officers, some of whom had served his father. He called himself a "little child" (1 Chron. 22:5; 29:1ff), a mark of both honesty and humility. The phrase "to go out or come in" refers to giving leadership to the nation (Num. 27:15-17; Deut. 31:2-3; 1 Sam. 18:13, 16; 2 Kings 11:8).

In his prayer, the king not only confessed his own smallness but also the nation's greatness (v. 8). The people of Israel were the people of God! This meant that God had a great purpose for them to fulfill on earth and that their king carried a great responsibility in ruling them. God had multiplied the nation and fulfilled His promise to Abraham (Gen. 12:2; 13:16; 15:5), Isaac (Gen. 26:1-5), and Jacob (Gen. 28:10-14), and Solomon wanted the blessing to continue.

The king concluded his prayer by anticipating the future and asking the Lord for the wisdom needed to rule the nation (v. 9). *Wisdom* was an important element in Near Eastern life and every king had his circle of "wise men" who advised him. But Solomon didn't ask for a committee of wise counselors; he asked for wisdom *for himself*. In that day, the wise person was one who was *skillful in the management of life.*[5] It meant much more than the ability to make a living; it meant the ability to make a life and make the most out of what life might bring. True wisdom involves skill in human relationships as well as the ability to understand and cooperate with the basic laws God has built into creation. Wise people not only have knowledge of human nature and of the created world, but they know how to use that knowledge in the right way at the right time. Wisdom isn't a theoretical idea or an abstract commodity; it's very practical and personal. There are many people who are smart enough to make a good living but they aren't wise enough to make a good life, a life of fulfillment that honors the Lord.

Solomon asked God to give him "an understanding heart," because no matter how smart the mind may be, if the heart is wrong, all of life will be wrong. "Keep your heart with all diligence, for out of it spring the issues of life" (Prov. 4:23, NKJV). The word translated "understanding" means "hearing"; Solomon wanted a "hearing heart." True understanding comes from hearing what God has to say, and to the Old Testament Jew, "hearing" meant "obeying." When the Lord speaks to us, it's not that we might study and pass judgment on what He said, *but that we might obey it.* An understanding heart has insight and exercises discernment. It is able to distinguish the things that differ (Phil. 1:9-11). It knows what is real and what is artificial, what is temporal and what is eternal.[6] This kind of understanding is described in Isaiah 11:1-5, a prophecy concerning the Messiah. Believers today can claim the promise of James 1:5.

Approbation (vv. 10-13). God was pleased with Solomon's request for wisdom, for it showed that the king was concerned with serving God and His people by knowing and doing God's will. Solomon never read Matthew 6:33, but he practiced it—and the Lord gave to him the additional blessings that he didn't ask for! God always gives His best to those who leave the choice with Him. When you read the Book of Proverbs, you find that the love of wisdom and the practice of discernment can lead to these extra blessings (see Prov. 3:1-2, 10, 13-18). In the subsequent chapters, we will learn about Solomon's wealth and honor and how he attracted visitors from other nations who wanted to hear his wisdom.

Obligation (v. 14). The Lord was careful to remind Solomon that his obedience to God's covenant and his devotion to the

Lord were the keys to his future blessings. Solomon was required to write out his own personal copy of Deuteronomy (Deut. 17:18-20), and this would include the covenant spelled out in Deuteronomy 28–30. Solomon also knew the terms of the covenant God made with his father David (2 Sam. 7:1-17) and that it required obedience on the part of David's son and successor (vv. 12-16). God promised to lengthen Solomon's life if he obeyed the Word (Prov. 3:2, 16), for he would be honoring God and his father David and could claim the promise of Exodus 20:12 (see Eph. 6:1-3). It's unfortunate that Solomon with all his wisdom forgot this part of the agreement and gradually drifted into sin and disobedience, and God had to chasten him.[7]

When Solomon returned to Jerusalem, he went to the tent that housed the ark and there offered more sacrifices (v. 15). The ark represented the presence of God among His people and the rule of God over His people (Pss. 80:1; 99:1). Solomon acknowledged the sovereign rule of God over his own life and the life of the nation. In other words, Solomon knew that he was second in command. It was when he started to forget that basic truth that he got himself into trouble.

4. The discerner (1 Kings 3:16-28)
God's chosen leaders can't always remain on the heights of spiritual glory but must take that glory and blessing with them into the place of duty and service. Jesus left the Mount of Transfiguration for the valley of conflict (Matt. 17:1-21), and Paul left the heights of heaven to carry on earth the pain of a thorn in the flesh (2 Cor. 12:1-10). Solomon had been worshiping at Gibeon and Jerusalem, but now he has returned to the responsibilities of the throne.

Like his father David, Solomon gave the common people access to the king (2 Sam. 14). God had given Solomon a special gift of wisdom and now he could put it to use. He had stood before the ark, the throne of God, and now his people could stand before his throne and seek help. But for Solomon to receive two prostitutes at his throne was certainly an act of condescension. Like Jesus, he welcomed "publicans and sinners" (Luke 15:1-2), except that Jesus did more than solve their problems: He changed their hearts and forgave their sins. In every way, Jesus is "greater than Solomon"(Matt. 12:42).

Although prostitution seemed to be tolerated in Israel, the Law of Moses laid down some severe restrictions and punishments (Lev. 19:29; 21:7, 9, 14; Deut. 23:18.) The Book of Proverbs warned young men about the wiles of the harlot ("the strange woman") and Paul instructed believers to avoid prostitutes (1 Cor. 6:15-16). These two women lived together with other prostitutes in a brothel, they became pregnant about the same time and both delivered babies. One can't help but feel sorry for the little ones who came into the world in such a place, without fathers to provide for them and protect them. But the kind of men who would visit prostitutes might not be the best fathers!

Since there were no witnesses to the birth of the two babies or the death of the one, the case couldn't be tried in the courts in the normal way. It would be one woman's word against the word of the other, even though it was obvious that one of the women was a liar. Using the divine wisdom God gave him, Solomon bypassed the word of the women and went right to their hearts, for the heart of every problem is the problem in the heart. By suggesting that they "divide the baby" between them, Solomon revealed the heart of the true mother and gave her baby to her. We aren't told what he did with the mother who had lied and stolen (kidnapped) the baby. We trust that the true mother abandoned her sinful ways and raised her son in the ways of the Lord.

For weeks, the account of this event was the main topic of conversation in all Israel, and Solomon's decision announced to everybody that the king was indeed a wise man.

5. The administrator (1 Kings 4:1-28; 2 Chron. 1:14-17)
David was a gifted administrator (2 Sam. 8:15-18; 20:23-26) and his son inherited some of that ability. Even though Solomon had great wisdom and authority, he couldn't handle the affairs of the kingdom alone. A good leader chooses capable associates and

allows them to use their own gifts and thereby serve the Lord and the people.

Special officers (vv. 1-6). Azariah was the high priest (v. 2). He was the son of Ahimaaz and the grandson of Zadok, the priest who had served David so faithfully. It appears that Ahimaaz had died and therefore his son was given the office. See 2 Samuel 15:27, 36; 1 Chron. 6:8-9. The word *ben* in Hebrew can mean son or grandson. While David had only one scribe, Solomon had two (v. 3), and they were the sons of David's scribe, Shisha. He was also known as Seriah (2 Sam. 8:17), Sheva (2 Sam. 20:25) and Shavsha (1 Chron. 18:16). Solomon's kingdom was much larger and more complex than that over which his father ruled, so the keeping of records would have been more demanding.

Jehoshaphat had been recorder during David's reign (2 Sam. 8:16; 20:24), and Benaiah had been appointed head of the army by Solomon (2:35). He was born into a priestly family but chose a military life instead. Abiathar had been exiled because of his part in the plot involving Adonijah (2:27), and Zadok had died and been replaced by his grandson. Since both Zadok and Abiathar had served with David, they are found in the official roster. Azariah was in charge of the twelve officers who supervised the twelve districts that Solomon had marked out in Israel (vv. 7-19). Whether his father was Nathan the prophet (1:11), Nathan the son of David (2 Sam. 5:14), or another man named Nathan is not explained. Nathan was a popular name in Israel.

Zabud was a priest who served as special adviser to the king; Ahishar managed the complex affairs of the king's household; and Adoniram was in charge of the men who were drafted to labor in the public works of the kingdom (9:15-23; 2 Chron. 2:2, 17-18; 8:7-10). These would not be Israelites but foreigners in the land. However, in the building of the temple, Solomon did conscript Israelites to devote four months a year to public service (5:13-18). Adoniram was also known as Adoram and he was stoned to death by the people when Rehoboam became king (1 Kings 12:18-20). Samuel had warned the people that their king would do such things (1 Sam. 8:12-18).

Special commissioners (vv. 7-19, 27-28). Solomon marked out twelve "districts" of various sizes and put a commissioner over each district. The boundaries of the districts ignored the traditional boundaries of the tribes and even incorporated territory that David had taken in battle, and each district was to provide food for the king's household for one month. It's likely that the commissioners also collected taxes and supervised the recruiting of soldiers and laborers for the temple and Solomon's other building projects. By establishing new districts that crossed over old boundaries, Solomon may have hoped to minimize tribal loyalty and eliminate some of the tension between Judah and the northern tribes. Instead, the plan only aggravated the tension, particularly since Judah wasn't included in the redistricting program. Being the royal tribe that contained the royal city, Judah was administered separately.

Any king with seven hundred wives and three hundred concubines, plus numerous officers and frequent guests, would have a large household to feed. The Queen of Sheba came with "a very great train" that must have included several hundred people. According to verses 22-23, the meals for one day in the palace required 185 bushels of fine flour, 375 bushels of coarse meal, ten oxen fattened in the stall and twenty oxen from the pasture, one hundred sheep, and various kind of game and fowl. Solomon also needed grain for his many horses, which may have been how the coarse meal (barley) was used. The conquered nations may have looked upon these monthly donations as part of their tribute to King Solomon, but the Jewish tribes considered the whole system to be an humiliating form of extortion. After Solomon's death, it was no wonder that the ten tribes rose up in revolt against "all the king's horses and all the king's men."

For some reason, five of the commissioners are identified by their fathers, for *ben* in Hebrew means "son of" (8-11, 13). The son of Abinadab (v. 11) may have been a son of David's own brother and therefore a cousin to Solomon (1 Sam. 16:8; 17:13). He also married one of Solomon's daughters, as also did Ahimaaz (v. 15). It's likely that Solomon instituted this supply system several years into his reign since he didn't have adult children when he was crowned. Baana was probably a brother to Jehoshaphat the recorder (vv. 12 and 3). These twelve men had great power in the land and were a part of the corrupt bureaucracy that Solomon wrote about in Ecclesiastes 5:8-12.

Special disctinctions (vv. 20-28). The nation of Israel became famous for its large population, its peace and security, its buildings, its wise king, and its satisfying lifestyle, "eating, and drinking, and making merry" (v. 20, KJV). Of course, the population grew because of God's promise to the patriarchs (Gen. 15:5; 17:8; 22:17; 26:4; 32:12) and His promises in the covenant (Deut. 28:1-14). The enlarged territory was also a part of God's promise (Gen. 15:18; Ex. 23:31; Deut. 1:7; Josh. 1:4). The tributary nations submitted to Solomon's rule and brought him gifts and tribute annually, and Solomon enjoyed great blessing because of God's covenant with David (2 Sam. 7). Contrary to God's law, Solomon multiplied horses in the land (Deut. 17:16) and built special cities for housing them (v. 26; 10:26-29; 2 Chron. 1:14-17; 9:25, 28).[8]

6. The scholar (1 Kings 4:29-34)

King David appreciated and enjoyed God's created world and wrote hymns of praise about the Creator and His creation, but Solomon looked upon nature more as an object of study. God gave Solomon wisdom and breadth of understanding beyond that of the great wise men of the east, and he was able to lecture accurately about the living things in God's creation. Ecclesiastes 2:5 informs us that Solomon planted great gardens, and no doubt it was in these that he observed the way plants and trees developed.

Ethan and Heman are mentioned in 1 Chronicles 15:19 as members of David's musical staff assigned to direct sanctuary worship. Ethan is probably the man also known as Jeduthun who wrote Psalms 39 and 89 (1 Chron. 16:41-42; 25:1, 6), and Psalm 88 is assigned to Heman. These men were also known for their wisdom. Other than 1 Chronicles 2:6, we have no further information about Calcol and Darda.

Most of Solomon's three thousand proverbs have been lost, for fewer than six hundred are recorded in the Book of Proverbs. Also lost are "the annals of Solomon" (11:41) as well as the books about Solomon written by Nathan, Ahijah, and Iddo (2 Chron. 9:29). We do find many references to nature in Proverbs, Ecclesiastes, and the Song of Solomon, so Solomon's scientific enquiries did yield spiritual truth and practical lessons for life. He became an international celebrity and important people from all over the known world came to see his treasures and hear his wisdom.

Peace and prosperity reigned while Solomon was king, but no matter how successful things appeared to citizens and visitors, all was not well in the kingdom. During the period between his ascension to the throne and his dedication of the temple, Solomon appears to have walked with the Lord and sought to please him. But Alexander Whyte expressed it vividly when he wrote that "the secret worm . . . was gnawing all the time in the royal staff upon which Solomon leaned."[9] Solomon didn't have the steadfast devotion to the Lord that characterized his father, and his many pagan wives were planting seeds in his heart that would bear bitter fruit.

THREE

1 KINGS 5:1–6:38; 7:13-51
[2 CHRONICLES 2–4]

Fulfilling David's Dream

"Surely I will not come into the tabernacle of my house, nor go up into my bed; I will not give sleep to mine eyes or slumber to mine eyelids, until I find out a place for the Lord, an habitation for the mighty God of Jacob" (Ps. 132:3-5, KJV). So wrote King David, for it was his passionate desire to build a temple for the glory of the Lord. "One thing have I desired of the Lord, that will I seek after; that I may dwell in the house of the Lord all the days of my life, to behold the beauty of the Lord, and to inquire in his temple" (Ps. 27:4, KJV).

The Lord knew David's heart but made it clear that He had other plans for His beloved servant (2 Sam. 7). David was so busy fighting wars and expanding and defending the borders of the kingdom of Israel that he didn't have time to supervise such a complex and demanding enterprise. Solomon, the man of peace, was God's choice to build the temple, and his father prepared him for the task and encouraged him (1 Chron. 22 and 28).

Since the days of Moses, the people of Israel had brought their sacrifices and offerings to the tabernacle, but now they were no longer a pilgrim people but a nation settled in their own land. The tabernacle was a fragile, portable building, and the time had

37

come for Israel to build a temple to their great God. The nations around them had temples dedicated to their false gods, so it was only right that the people of Israel dedicate a magnificent temple to honor Jehovah of Hosts, the true and living God. In the second month (our April/May) of the year 966, the fourth year of his reign, Solomon began the work,[1] and these chapters record several stages of the project.

1. Securing the materials (1 Kings 5:1-12; 2 Chron. 2:1-16)

As he anticipated the building of the temple, David had set aside some of the spoils of battle especially for the Lord (1 Chron. 22:14). This amounted to 3,750 tons of gold, 37,500 tons of silver, and an unmeasured amount of bronze, iron, wood, and stone. All this wealth he presented publicly to Solomon (1 Chron. 29:1-5). David also added his own personal treasure and then invited the leaders of the nation to contribute as well (1 Chron. 29:1-10). The final totals were 4,050 tons of gold and over 38,000 tons of silver, not to speak of thousands of tons of bronze and iron, as well as precious stones. It was a great beginning for a great project.

David also gave Solomon the plans for the temple that had been given to him by the Lord (1 Chron. 28). David had also assembled some artisans and laborers to follow those plans and work in wood and stone to prepare material for the temple (1 Chron. 22:1-4). Hiram, king of Tyre, had provided workers and materials for the building of David's palace (2 Sam. 5:11), and David had enlisted their help in preparing wood for the temple (1 Chron. 22:4). Solomon took advantage of this royal friendship to enlist Hiram to provide the workers and timber needed for the temple.

Hiram had sent Solomon his greetings on the occasion of his coronation, and Solomon had sent back official thanks plus a request for his help in the construction of the temple. In his message, Solomon indicated that he knew that his father had discussed the building of the temple with Hiram, so Hiram wasn't hearing about it for the first time. David had even told Hiram about God's covenant (2 Sam. 7) and God's choice of Solomon to build the house of God. Solomon made it clear that he was constructing, not a monument to the glory of his father, but a temple to the honor of the name of the Lord (v. 5; see 8:16-20, 29, 33, 35, 41-44).

Solomon also requested a master artisan who could make the intricate and beautiful furnishings required for the temple (7:13-14; 2 Chron. 2:7), and King Hiram sent him Hiram (or Huram-Abi; 2 Chron. 2:13-14). He was the son of a mixed marriage, for his father was a Phoenician and his mother was from the tribe of Naphtali.[2] He was gifted as a metal worker and cast the two pillars at the entrance of the temple as well as the metal furnishings within the temple. As when Moses built the tabernacle, the Lord assembled the needed workers and empowered them to do their work (Ex. 31:1-11; 35:30-35).

Solomon's letter was really a commercial contract, for in it he offered to pay for the wood by providing food annually for Hiram's household (5:11), and also to pay the workers one large payment for their labor (2 Chron. 2:10). Until the work was completed, King Hiram's household received annually 125,000 bushels of wheat and 115,000 gallons of pure olive oil. The workers would receive one payment of 125,000 bushels of wheat, 125,000 bushels of barley, and 115,000 gallons of wine and of olive oil, all of which would be divided among them. In his reply, Hiram accepted the terms and outlined the procedure. His men would cut the trees in Lebanon, prepare the logs, and then take them down the coast to Joppa (modern Jaffa; 2 Chron. 2:16), either on ships or bound together as rafts. At Joppa Solomon's men would claim the timber and transport it overland to the building site, about thirty-five miles away, as the crow flies.[3]

As any pastor and church board can attest, building programs are not easy, and they either bring out the best or the worst in God's people. But like Moses who supervised the building of the tabernacle, Solomon had a great deal going for him. Both men knew that God had chosen them to direct the work and that He would enable them to finish successfully. Both leaders had an incredible amount of wealth and materials at their disposal before they started, and both received the construction plans from the Lord Himself. Both were blessed to have leaders who gave generously to support the project.

2. Conscripting workers (1 Kings 5:13-18; 9:15-23; 2 Chron. 2:2, 17-18; 8:7-10)
It would take a great deal of manpower to fell the trees, trim the logs, and transport them to the construction site for the builders to use. David's incomplete census had revealed that there were 1,300,000 able-bodied men in the land (2 Sam. 24:9) and Solomon conscripted only 30,000 to labor on the temple, about 2.3 percent of the total available labor force. Ten thousand of the men spent one month each quarter in Lebanon assisting Hiram's men in their work, and then they had two months at home. These men were Jewish citizens and were not treated like slaves (9:22; see Lev. 25:39-43). We aren't told if they shared in any of the wages Solomon promised Hiram's workers, but they probably didn't.

Solomon also took a census of the non-Israelite aliens in the land and drafted 150,000 of them to cut and transport stones for the temple (5:15-18; 9:15-23; 2 Chron. 2:17-18; 8:7-10). Of this group, 70,000 carried burdens and 80,000 cut limestone blocks from the hills. In charge of this group were 3,000 overseers and 300 supervisors who were aliens, and over the entire group were 250 Jewish officers. The stone blocks had to be cut carefully so they would fit together perfectly when assembled at the temple site (6:7), and that would demand careful planning and expert supervision.

Even though the conscription involved a very small portion of the male citizens, the Jewish people resented Solomon taking 30,000 of their men to work in Lebanon four months out of the year. This critical attitude helped to strengthen the people's revolt against Rehoboam and to precipitate the division of the nation after Solomon's death (12:1-21). Indeed, when it came to labor and taxes, Solomon did indeed put a heavy yoke on the people.

Both Jews and Gentiles assisted in the construction of the temple, and this fact is significant, for the temple was to be "a house of prayer for all nations" (Isa. 56:7; Matt. 21:13; Luke 19:46). After the captivity, the Persian government assisted the Jews in rebuilding their temple, and Herod's temple had a special area for the Gentiles. Sad to say, some of the Jewish religious leaders turned the court of the Gentiles into a market for selling sacrifices and changing foreign money into Jewish currency. The church today is a temple of God composed of believers in Jesus Christ, both Jews and Gentiles (Eph. 2:11-22). It is being "built up" to the glory of the Lord as "living stones"—both Jews and Gentiles—are added to the temple by the Holy Spirit (1 Peter 2:5).

Hiram's workmen in Lebanon were not worshipers of the Lord, and the aliens in the land of Israel were not Jewish proselytes, yet God used both of these groups of "outsiders" to help build His holy temple. The Lord would "have all men to be saved" (1 Tim. 2:4, KJV), but even if they aren't believers, He can use them to fulfill His purposes. He used Nebuchadnezzar and the Babylonian army to chasten Israel, and called Nebuchadnezzar "my servant" (Jer. 25:9), and He used Cyrus king of Persia to set Israel free and help them rebuild their temple (Ezra 1). This should encourage us in our praying and serving, for the Lord can use people we least appreciate to get His will done on earth. God can even work through unconverted government officials to open doors for His people or meet the needs they might have.

3. Building the temple (1 Kings 6:1-38; 2 Chron. 3:1-17)

What were David's two greatest sins? Most people would reply, "His adultery with Bathsheba and his taking a census of the people," and their answers would be correct. As a result of his sin of numbering the people, David purchased property on Mount Moriah where he built an altar and worshiped the Lord (2 Sam. 24). David married Bathsheba and God gave them a son whom they named Solomon (2 Sam. 12:24-25). Now we have Solomon building a temple on David's property on Mount Moriah! God took the consequences of David's two worst sins—a piece of property and a son—and built a temple! "But where sin abounded, grace abounded much more" (Rom. 5:20, NKJV). This isn't an encouragement for us to sin, because David paid dearly for both of those transgressions, but it is an encouragement to us go on serving God after we've repented and confessed our sins. Satan wants us to think that all is lost, but the God of all grace is still at work (1 Peter 5:10).

The outer structure (vv. 1-10, 36-38; 2 Chron. 3). The ancient world had a "short cubit" or "common cubit" of almost eighteen inches and a "long cubit" of almost twenty-one inches. The common cubit was used for the temple (2 Chron. 3:3), which means that the structure was ninety feet long, thirty feet wide, and forty-five feet high. A porch thirty feet wide and fifteen feet deep stood at the front of the temple, and a courtyard for the priests surrounded the sanctuary. It was separated from an outer courtyard by a wall composed of stone blocks and wood (v. 36; 2 Chron. 4:9). Jeremiah 36:10 calls the court of the priests "the upper courtyard," which suggests that it stood higher than the outer courtyard. The doors of the temple faced east, as did the gate of the tabernacle.

Unlike the tabernacle, the temple had three levels of rooms attached to outer walls of the temple on the south, west, and north walls. Each chamber was 7 and a half feet high. The walls that supported these chambers were constructed like three stairsteps, and the chambers stood on wooden supports that rested on these stairs. The rooms on the upper lever were ten and a half feet wide, on the second level nine feet wide, and on the lowest level seven and a half feet wide. These chambers were probably used for storage. At the middle of the south wall of the temple was a door leading to the lowest level of rooms and to a spiral stairway leading to the middle and top floors. On each level there must have been a narrow passage connecting the rooms. In the north and south walls, above the third level of rooms, were narrow windows that let in a small amount of light (v. 4). There were no windows in the tabernacle of Moses. However, the light necessary for ministry in the holy place came from ten lampstands, five along the north wall and five along the south wall. Of course, so large and heavy a structure required a strong foundation (v. 38).

A divine message (vv.11-13). We don't know who brought this message (probably a prophet) or when it was delivered, but the Lord sent His Word to the king at a time when he was either discouraged with the building program or (more likely) starting to become proud of what he was accomplishing. The Lord reminded Solomon, as He must constantly remind us, that He's not impressed with our work if our walk isn't obedient to Him. What He wants is an obedient heart (Eph. 6:6). God would fulfill His promises to David and Solomon (2 Sam. 7), not because Solomon built the temple but because he obeyed the Word of the Lord. A similar warning was included in the covenant God gave Moses in Deuteronomy 28–30, so it was not a new revelation to Solomon. This was the second time God spoke to Solomon about obedience (see 3:5ff), and He would speak to him about it again after the dedication of the temple (9:3-9).

The inner structure (vv. 14-35). When the basic building was completed, the workers focused on the inside of the temple, which was the most important part, for it was there that the priests carried out the ministry of the Lord. The interior walls from ceiling to floor were paneled with cedar boards, overlaid with gold (v. 22), on which were carved open flowers and gourds, and the floor was covered with planks of pine (or fir), also overlaid with gold (vv. 15 and 30). A pair of beautifully carved folding doors led into the Holy Place from the court of the priests (vv. 31-35). Like the cherubim, these doors were made of olivewood covered with gold, and they even had hinges of gold (7:50). Golden chains hung across the outside of the doors (v. 21).

At the west end of the Holy Place, sixty feet from the doors, hung the beautiful veil that marked off the Holy of Holies, also called the most Holy Place (2 Chron. 3:10). This created a room that was a cube, measuring thirty feet on every side (v. 20).[4] In the tabernacle of Moses, the Holy of Holies was also a cube, but it measured only fifteen feet per side. In fact, the dimensions of the temple were twice those of the tabernacle—90 feet by 30 feet as opposed to 45 feet by 15 feet. The walls of the Holy of Holies were paneled with cedar wood and covered with gold, and the floor was made of gold-plated fir planks. Even the nails used in the Holy of Holies were plated with gold. In was in the Holy of Holies that the ark of the covenant was kept.

The ark of the covenant represented the throne of God who was "enthroned between the cherubim" (Ps. 80:1, NIV). It was a wooden chest, forty-five inches long, twenty-seven inches wide, and twenty-seven inches high. Because the two tables of the law were in the ark, it was also called "the ark of the testimony" (Ex. 25:22). Across the top of the ark was a golden "mercy seat," and at each end was a cherub made of olive wood and covered with gold. The cherbim were fifteen feet high and their wings were fifteen feet across, so that as the ark sat in the Holy of Holies, the four wings reached from wall to wall. (See vv. 23-28 and Ex. 25:10-22 and 37:1-9). Once a year, the high priest was permitted to enter the Holy of Holies, sprinkle the blood of the sacrifice on the mercy seat and thus cover the sins of the people for another year (Lev. 16).

Hiram cast two large pillars of bronze, each twenty-seven feet high and eighteen feet in circumference.[5] They were freestanding, about four inches thick and hollow (Jer. 52:21). A decorative capital 4_ feet high rested on top of each pillar (2 Kings 25:17). It was comprised of an inverted bowl, lotus petals, and a network or interwoven chain of pomegranates. The two pillars were named "Jachin" ("he establishes") and "Boaz" ("in him is strength") and they stood outside the entrance to the Holy Place, Jachin to the north and Boaz to the south. The "he" in these definitions surely refers to God, and the pillars bore witness to the Jewish people that it was God who established their nation and Israel's faith in Jehovah was the source of their strength. Some see in this a reference to David's dynasty, established by God (2 Sam. 7) and continued by Him.

4. Furnishing the temple (1 Kings 7:13-51; 2 Chron. 4)
The furnishings of the temple were important to the priests, for

without the divinely ordained furniture, they couldn't do their ministry or please the Lord.

The brazen altar (2 Chron. 4:1). As you approached the temple from the east, you came to the entrance to the inner courtyard of the priests. It was to this entrance that the people brought their sacrifices and offerings to be presented to the Lord. On the right, toward the north, stood the altar of brass, thirty feet square and fifteen feet high (2 Chron. 4:1), where the fire was kept burning and the priests offered the sacrifices (see 8:64; 9:25; see Ex. 27:1-8; 38:1-7). The height of the altar suggests that there must have been steps leading up to a ledge on which the priests could stand and minister (see Ezek. 43:13-17). Some students believe that the altar itself wasn't fifteen feet high but was shorter than that and stood on a stone base that raised it higher. The tabernacle altar was only four and a half feet high.

The laver or molten sea (vv. 23-26; 2 Chron. 4:2-5, 10). To the left of the entrance, on the south side of the court (v. 39), stood the huge "molten sea" that replaced the smaller laver that had stood in the tabernacle court (vv. 23-26; see Ex. 30:17-21; 38:8). It was round and made of brass a handbreadth thick with the image of lilies around the rim, and it could hold over 17,000 gallons of water.[6] This large basin measured fifteen feet across and was seven and a half feet high. It stood on the backs of twelve cast statues of oxen, in groups of three, with each group facing a different direction. Perhaps these twelve oxen represented the twelve tribes of Israel. (See 2 Kings 16:17.)

There must have been a system for removing small amounts of water so the priests could wash their hands and feet, but this system isn't explained in the text. Perhaps there were spigots at the base of the basin. If the priests didn't keep their hands and feet clean as they ministered in the temple, they were in danger of death (Ex. 30:20). In Scripture, water for drinking is a picture of the Spirit of God (John 7:37-39), while water for washing is a picture of the Word of God (Ps. 119:9; John 15:3; Eph. 5:25-27). As the priests labored for the Lord in the temple, they became defiled and needed to be cleansed; and as we serve the Lord, we too can become defiled and need the "washing of water by the word." Jesus pictured this truth in John 13 when He washed the disciples' feet.

The ten stands and lavers (vv. 27-39; 2 Chron. 4:6). These were beautifully decorated metal wagons, six feet square and four and a half feet high, with handles at each corner. Each stand could hold a basin that held 230 gallons of water. The stands were kept in the court of the priests right next to the sanctuary, five on the north side and five on the south side. Since the stands were on wheels, they could easily be moved from place to place. They were used for the washing and preparing of the sacrifices (2 Chron. 4:6) and perhaps for the general cleanliness of the temple. The dirty water could then be wheeled away and disposed of in a proper place and the basins filled with clean water from the molten sea.

It's worth noting that these very practical and useful stands were also very beautiful, which teaches us that God sees beauty in holiness and the holiness of beauty (Ex. 28:2; Pss. 29:2; 96:6, 9; 110:3).

The golden incense altar (6:20, 22; 7:48). The altar was made of cedar covered with gold, but we have no dimensions given in the text. It stood before the veil that separated the Holy Place from the Holy of Holies, and on it the priests burned incense each morning and evening when they cared for the lamps (Ex. 30:1-10; 37:25-29). In Scripture, the burning of incense is a picture of our prayers rising up to the Lord (Ps. 141:1-2; Rev. 5:8; Luke 1:8-10). The Lord gave Moses the recipe for the mixture of spices that was used in the tabernacle and temple worship (Ex. 30:34-38), and this mixture was not to be counterfeited or used for any other purpose. The golden altar was used for no other purpose, and on the annual Day of Atonement, the high priest applied blood to this altar to cleanse and purify it (Ex. 30:10). Without "clean hands and a pure heart" (Ps. 24:3-5), we can't approach the Lord and expect Him to hear and answer prayer (Ps. 66:18; Heb. 10:19-25).

The golden lampstands and tables (vv. 48-49; 2 Chron. 4:7-8, 19-20). In the tabernacle that Moses constructed, there was only one table for the loaves of bread, but the temple had ten golden tables, five in a line on each side of the Holy Place. The tabernacle had one golden lampstand with seven lamps on it, but the temple had ten golden lampstands in the Holy Place, five along the north wall and five along the south wall. They provided the light needed for the ministry in the Holy Place.

The miscellaneous utensils (vv. 40-50; 2 Chron. 4:7-8, 11-22). The priests required many different utensils in order to carry on their work, including wick trimmers, bowls for sprinkling water and sacrificial blood, dishes, ladles, large pots for cooking the meat from the peace offerings, and shovels for removing the ashes. The temple was an imposing structure that contained expensive furnishings made of gold and polished bronze, but the daily ministry would have been impossible without these small utensils.

It's difficult to calculate the cost of this building in modern currency. It isn't enough just to know the price of the precious metal today, but we also need to know its purchasing power. Then we must calculate what Solomon paid for manpower and materials and try to express it in contemporary equivalents. When you consider that there was gold overlay on the inside walls and floors, the furniture, the doors, and the cherubim, you have no hesitation concluding that this was a very costly building. And yet all this beauty was destroyed and this wealth was confiscated when the Babylonian army captured Jerusalem and destroyed the temple (see Jer. 52). Nebuchadnezzar robbed the temple and deported the captives in stages, and eventually his men burned the city and the temple so they could get their hands on all the gold that was there.

How painful it is to realize that Solomon, the man who constructed the temple, was the man who married a multitude of foreign wives and encouraged idolatry in Israel, the very sin that turned the nation away from God and brought upon them the fiery judgment of the Lord.

FOUR

1 KINGS 8:1–9:9, 25-28
[2 CHRONICLES 5–7]

God's House and Solomon's Heart

"Fellow citizens, we cannot escape history." Abraham Lincoln spoke those words to the American Congress on December 1, 1862, but King Solomon could have spoken them to the Jewish leaders when he dedicated the temple during the Feast of Tabernacles in the twenty-fourth year of his reign.[1] No matter where the Jews are in this world, or what the century is, they have their roots in Abraham, Moses, and David. King David is mentioned twelve times in this section[2] and Moses is mentioned three times. During his prayer, Solomon referred to God's covenant with his father (2 Sam. 7) and also to the covenant God gave to Moses recorded in Deuteronomy 28–30. The main thrust of his prayer is that God would hear the prayers directed toward the temple and forgive those who sinned, and this request is based on the promise given in Deuteronomy 30:1-10. Israel's kings were commanded to make their own copy of the Book of Deuteronomy (Deut. 17:18-20), and Solomon's many references to Deuteronomy indicate that he knew the book very well.

What kind of a "house" did Solomon dedicate that day?

1. A house of God (1 Kings 8:1-11; 2 Chron. 5:1-14)

Solomon assembled at Jerusalem the leaders of the tribes of Israel and whoever of the citizens could attend, from the north to south (v. 65), that they might assist him in dedicating the house of God. The word "house" is used twenty-six times in this passage (thirty-seven times in 2 Chron. 5–7), for this structure was indeed the "house of God." (vv. 10, 11, 17, etc.). But what made this costly building the house of the Lord? Not simply that God commanded it to be built and chose Solomon to build it, or that He gave the plans to David and provided the wealth to construct it. Those matters were important, but the thing that made this temple the house of the Lord was the presence of the Lord God Jehovah in the sanctuary.

The ark was brought in (vv. 1-9; 2 Chron. 5:1-9). In the Holy of Holies, Jehovah was "enthroned between the cherubim" (Ps. 80:1 NIV). The pagan nations had their temples, altars, priests and sacrifices, but their temples were empty and their sacrifices useless. The true and living God dwelt in the temple on Mount Moriah! That's why Solomon's first act of dedication was to have the ark of the covenant brought from the tent David had pitched for it (2 Sam. 6:17) and placed into the inner sanctuary of the temple.[3] The tabernacle equipment and furnishings were also brought to the temple and stored there (2 Chron. 5:5). The ark of the covenant was the only piece of the original furniture that was kept in active service, for nothing could replace the throne of God or the law of God that was kept in the ark. That this dedication service took place during the Feast of Tabernacles was significant, for the ark had led Israel all during their wilderness journey.

The priests placed the ark before the large cherubim that Hiram had made, whose wings spanned the width of the Holy of Holies (6:23-30). The cherubim on the original golden mercy seat looked at each other, while the new cherubim looked out toward the Holy Place where the priests ministered. The angels of God not only "look into" the mysteries of God's grace (1 Peter 1:12), but they also behold the ministry of God's people and learn about God's grace (1 Cor. 4:9; 11:10; Eph. 3:10; 1 Tim.

5:21). At one time, a pot of manna and the staff of Aaron stood before the ark (Ex. 16:33; Num. 17:10; Heb. 9:4), both of which were reminders of rebellion in Israel (Ex. 16:1-3; Num. 16). But the nation was now making a new beginning and those items weren't needed. The important thing was that Israel obey the law of God that was kept in the ark. The Jews were no longer a pilgrim people, but the staves were left in the ark as a reminder of God's faithfulness to them during those forty years of discipline.

The glory came down (vv. 10-11; 2 Chron. 5:11-14). The ark was but a symbol of the throne and presence of God; it was the actual presence of the Lord in His house that was important. Once Solomon and the people had honored God and placed His throne in the Holy of Holies, the glory of God came and filled the house of the Lord. The glory cloud had guided Israel through the wilderness (Num. 9:15-23), but now the glory came to dwell within the beautiful temple Solomon had built. As the glory filled the house, the priests praised God with voice and instruments, for the Lord inhabits the praises of His people (Ps. 22:3).

The presence of God's glory was the distinguishing mark of the nation of Israel (Ex. 33:12-23; Rom. 9:4). The sins of the people caused God's glory to depart from the tabernacle (1 Sam. 4:19-22), but now the glory had returned. But the nation would sin again and be taken to Babylon, and there Ezekiel the prophet would have a vision of the glory of God leaving the temple (Ezek. 8:1-4; 9:3; 10:4, 18-19; 11:22-23). However, God would also allow Ezekiel to see the glory return to the kingdom temple (43:1-5). The glory came to earth in the person of Jesus Christ (John 1:14; Matt. 17:1-7), but sinners crucified "the Lord of glory" (1 Cor. 2:8). When Jesus returned to heaven, the cloud of glory accompanied Him (Acts 1:9) and the temple was left "desolate" (Matt. 23:38–24:2).

Since the coming of the Spirit at Pentecost (Acts 2), God's glory has resided in each of God's children individually (1 Cor. 6:19-20) as well as in the church local (1 Cor. 3:16) and the church universal (Eph. 2:19-22). Until Jesus comes to take us to the eternal glory, our privilege and responsibility is to bring glory to Him as we serve here on earth. Each local assembly, worshiping the Lord in spirit and truth, should manifest the glory of the Lord (1 Cor. 14:23-25).

2. A house of testimony (1 Kings 8:12-21; 2 Chron. 6:1-11)

God not only graciously dwells with His people, but He also gives them His Word and faithfully keeps His promises. That's the major theme of this section, for in it Solomon glorified Jehovah by reviewing the history of the building of the temple.

The mystery of God (vv. 12-13; 2 Chron. 6:1-2). The king was standing on his special platform (2 Chron. 6:13), facing the sanctuary, the priests were at the altar (5:12) and the people were gathered in the assembly, and all of them had just seen a marvelous manifestation of the glory of God. Yet Solomon opened his address by saying, "The Lord said He would dwell in the dark cloud" (v. 12, NKJV). Why speak of darkness when they had just beheld God's radiant glory? Solomon was referring to the words of the Lord to Moses at Mount Sinai: "Behold, I come to you in the thick cloud, that the people may hear when I speak with you, and believe you forever" (Ex. 19:9, NKJV). There was indeed a thick cloud of darkness on the mountain (Ex. 19:16; 20:21; Deut. 4:11; 5:22) and Moses went into that darkness with great fear (Heb. 12:18-21). Solomon was connecting the events of that day to Israel's past experience at Sinai, for the people of God must not be cut off from their roots in history.

God is light (1 John 1:5) and dwells in light (1 Tim. 6:16), but He cannot fully reveal Himself to man because "there shall no man see me, and live" (Ex. 33:20, KJV). The emphasis at Sinai was on *hearing* God, not *seeing* God, lest the Jewish people would be tempted to make images of their God and worship them. Like the church today, Israel was to be a people of the Word, hearing it and obeying. King David envisioned the Lord with darkness under His feet and darkness as His canopy (Ps. 18:9, 11; see 97:2). There is mystery about God that humbles us, because we don't always understand Him and His ways, but this mystery also encourages us to trust Him and rest upon His Word. Solomon didn't want the people to think that God was now their "neighbor" and therefore they could speak to Him or about Him any way they pleased. "But the Lord is in His holy temple. Let all the earth be silent before Him" (Hab. 2:20, NASB).

Like a servant reporting to his master, Solomon announced that he had built the house to be God's dwelling place (v. 13). This reminds us that Moses finished work of building and erecting the tabernacle (Ex. 40:33), that our Savior finished all that the Father instructed Him to do (John 17:4), and that both John the Baptist and Paul finished their courses successfully (Acts 13:25; 2 Tim. 4:7). All of us will give an account of our life and service when we see the Lord (Rom. 14:10-13), and it behooves us to be faithful to the calling He has given us, so that we end well.

The goodness and faithfulness of God (vv. 15-21). Over more than fifty years of ministry, it's been my privilege to assist many local churches in dedicating new sanctuaries; and in my messages, I've tried to emphasize the work of God in the history of His people. As A. T. Pierson used to say, "History is His story." It's easy for new church members and new generations that come along to take for granted or forget the history of their church. The weekly Sabbath, the annual feasts (Lev. 23), and the presence of the temple would bear witness to the Jewish people, young and old, that Jehovah was their God. The word "remember" is used at least fourteen times in the Book of Deuteronomy because God didn't want His people to forget the lessons of the past.

God in His goodness and grace made a covenant with David concerning his family and his throne (2 Sam. 7), and He included in that covenant the promise of a son who would build the temple. What God spoke with His mouth, He accomplished with His hand (v. 15), and what He promised to David, He performed through Solomon (v. 20). But God did these things for the honor of His name, not for the glory of either David or Solomon (vv. 16-20). God's name is referred to at least fourteen times in Solomon's address and prayer. The king was careful to give God all the glory. Whenever the people would come to worship, they would remember that the goodness and faithfulness of the Lord made the temple possible.

3. A house of prayer (1 Kings 8:22-53; 2 Chron. 6:12-42)

According to 2 Chronicles 6:13, Solomon knelt on the special platform near the altar as he prayed this prayer, his hands lifted to heaven. Our traditional posture for prayer ("hands folded and eyes closed") was unknown to the Jews. Their posture was to look up by faith toward God in heaven (or toward the temple) and lift their open hands to show their poverty and their expectancy as they awaited the answer (v. 38, 54; Ex. 9:29, 33; Pss. 63:4; 88:9; 143:6). This practice was carried over into the early church (1 Tim. 2:8). The word "heaven" is found at least a dozen times in verses 22-54.

Solomon opened his prayer with praise and thanksgiving to the Lord, the covenant-making and covenant-keeping God. "There is no God like thee" (v. 23; compare Ex. 15:11 and Deut. 4:39). He then referred to God's covenant with his father David, the covenant that appointed Solomon as David's heir and the builder of the temple (2 Sam. 7). But Solomon also claimed the covenant promise of the Davidic dynasty and prayed that David's royal line would continue just as God had promised. Of course, the ultimate fulfillment of that promise is in Jesus Christ (Luke 1:26-33, 67-75; Acts 2:29-30; Rom. 1:3).

As Solomon prayed, he was overwhelmed by the contrast between the greatness of God and the insignificance of the work he had done in building the temple. How could Almighty God, the God of the heavens, dwell in a building made by men's hands? Solomon had expressed this same truth to King Hiram before he began to build (2 Chron. 2:6, and the prophet Isaiah echoed it (Isa. 66:1). Stephen referred to these words from Solomon and Isaiah when he defended himself before the Jewish council (Acts 7:47-50), and Paul emphasized this truth when preaching to the Gentiles (Acts 17:24). Solomon realized that God's willingness to dwell with His people was wholly an act of grace.

The burden of his prayer is in verses 28-30: that the Lord would keep His eyes on the temple and His ears open to the prayers of the people and answer them when they prayed toward the temple. He asked the Lord to forgive the sins of the people when they prayed (vv. 30, 34, 36, 39, 50) and in so doing maintain "the cause of his people Israel" (v. 59). Solomon knew the terms of the covenant found in Deuteronomy 28–29, and the calamities he mentioned in his prayer are the very disciplines the Lord promised to send if Israel disobeyed His law. But Solomon also knew that Deuteronomy 30 promised forgiveness and restoration if God's people would repent and turn to the Lord. Jonah looked toward the temple and prayed, and God forgave him (Jonah 2:4), and Daniel prayed for the people as he looked toward Jerusalem (Dan. 6:10). "My house shall be called a house of prayer for all nations" (Isa. 56:7, NKJV; Matt. 21:13; Mark 11:17; Luke 19:46).

Solomon presented the Lord seven specific requests.

(1) Justice in the land (vv. 31-32; 2 Chron. 6:22-23). Solomon had begun his reign by judging between two women (3:16-28), but it would be impossible for him to handle every case of personal conflict in the land and still perform all the duties of the king. Judges were appointed in Israel to hear local cases (Ex. 18:13-27; 21:5-6; 22:7-12; Deut. 17:2-13; 25:1), and the priests were also available to apply the law and render decisions (1 Chron. 23:4; 26:29). If a man was accused of sinning against his neighbor, the accused could take an oath at the temple altar and the Lord would declare whether or not the man was innocent. How this verdict was declared isn't explained, but perhaps the priest used the Urim and Thummim (Ex. 28:30; Lev. 8:8). Justice in the land is essential if citizens are to enjoy "life, liberty, and the pursuit of happiness." How tragic that, in later years, it was the godless kings of Israel and Judah who allowed injustice into the land.

The judges' responsibility was to "condemn the wicked . . . and justify the righteous," but when it comes to our salvation, God justifies the ungodly (Rom. 4:5) on the basis of the sacrifice Christ made on the cross (Rom. 5:6). God has condemned all people as unrighteous (Rom. 3:23) so that He might show grace to all mankind and save those who will put their trust in His Son.

(2) Military defeat (vv. 33-34; 2 Chron. 6:24-25). This defeat is caused because the people have sinned in some way (Josh. 7) and the Lord is displeased with them. If Israel obeyed the terms of the covenant, there would be peace in the land and God would give Israel victory over any enemies who attacked them. But if Israel sinned, God would allow their enemies to triumph over them (Lev. 26:6-8, 14-17, 25, 33, 36-39; Deut. 28:1, 7, 15, 25-26, 49-52). If this defeat brought the people to repentance, then God would forgive them and see to it that the prisoners were released and returned home.

(3) Drought in the land (vv. 35-36; 2 Chron. 6:26-27). Israel had title to the land because of God's covenant with Abraham, but they could possess it and enjoy its blessings only if they obeyed God's law. One of the severest disciplines listed in the covenant was drought in the land (Lev. 26:19; Deut. 28:22-24, 48). The Lord promised His people that He would send the rain in its season (Deut. 11:10-14) only if they honored Him. Since the Israelites were a pastoral and agricultural people, rain was absolutely necessary for their survival. Whenever the people obeyed the Lord, they enjoyed bumper crops and their flocks and herds were healthy and multiplied. The purpose of drought was to bring the people to a place of repentance, and God promised to forgive their sins and send the rain. See 1 Kings 18.

(4) Other natural calamities (vv. 37-40; 2 Chron. 6:28-31).[4] God warned in the covenant that Israel's disobedience would bring divine discipline to them. He would send famine (Lev. 26:26, 29; Deut. 28:17, 48), blight (Lev. 26:20; Deut. 28:18, 22, 30, 39-40), invasions of insects (Deut. 28:38, 42), and various sicknesses and plagues (Lev. 26:16, 25; Deut. 28:21-22, 27, 35, 59-61). However, if they obeyed Him, He would shelter His people and their land from these calamities. But once again, Solomon asked the Lord to forgive His people when they confessed their sins, and to restore their land (see 2 Chron. 7:13-14).

In his prayer, Solomon frequently mentioned the land (vv. 34,

36-37, 40-41, 46-48) because this was part of Israel's inheritance from the Lord. When the people began to sin, God punished them first *in the land* (see the Book of Judges), and when they persisted in their rebellion, He allowed enemy nations to take them *out of the land*. In 722 B.C., the Assyrians conquered Israel and assimilated the people, and in 606–586 the Babylonians defeated Judah, burned Jerusalem and the temple, and took many of the people captive to Babylon. When God punished His people out of their land, He finally cured them of their idolatry.

(5) Foreigners who came to pray (vv. 41-43; 2 Chron. 6:32-33). These were not the "resident aliens" in Israel who settled in the land and had certain privileges and responsibilities under the law (Lev. 16:29; 17:10, 12; 18:26; 19:34; 20:2; 25:6, 45). The "foreigners" were people who would come to Israel because they had heard of the greatness of the Lord and His temple. (Gentile workers had helped to build the temple.) It was the responsibility of Israel to be a "light" to the pagan Gentile nations and to demonstrate to them the glory of the true and living God. Solomon had this in mind when he asked the Lord to hear and answer the prayers of people outside the covenant, so that "all peoples of the earth may know Your name and fear You" (v. 43 NKJV; see v. 60). If these people began to pray to the Lord Jehovah, perhaps they would come to trust and worship Him.

From the very beginning of the nation, when God called Abraham and Sarah to leave Ur and go to Canaan, God declared that He wanted Israel to be a blessing to the whole world (Gen. 12:1-3). God's judgments against Pharaoh and Egypt were a witness to the nations (Ex. 9:16), as was His opening of the Red Sea at the Exodus (Josh. 2:8-13). When God dried up the Jordan so Israel could enter the Promised Land, He revealed His power and glory to the other nations (Josh. 4:23-24). His blessing on Israel in the land of Canaan was a witness to the pagan nations (Deut. 28:7-14), and so was David's victory over Goliath (1 Sam. 17:46). God blesses us that we might be a blessing, not that we might horde the blessing and boast. The Jews prayed, "God be merciful to us and bless us, and cause His face to shine upon us, that Your way may be known on earth, Your salvation among all nations" (Ps. 67:1-2, NKJV). The church today needs to pray that prayer and keep that purpose in mind.

(6) *Armies in battle (vv. 44-45; 2 Chron. 6:34-35)*. When God sent His people into battle, it was a "holy war" that could be won only by His strength and wisdom. Using the silver trumpets, the priests sounded the call to arms (2 Chron. 13:12-16; Num. 10:1-10). They assisted the armies to ascertain God's will (1 Sam. 23:1-2), and they encouraged the men to fight for the glory of the Lord and trust Him alone (Deut. 20:1-4). Even in the midst of battle, the soldiers could look toward the temple and ask the Lord for His help. When he described the Christian soldier's equipment, Paul included prayer as one of the essentials for victory (Eph. 6:18-19). The French writer Voltaire said, "It is said that God is always on the side of the heaviest battalions," but the truth is that God is on the side of those who pray in His will.

(7) *Defeat and captivity (vv. 46-53; 2 Chron. 6:36-39)*. The pronoun "they" in verse 46 refers to the people of Israel, and Israel's history shows that the nation was prone to sin. All of us are sinners (Prov. 20:9; Rom. 3:23), but God's special blessings on Israel and His covenant with them made their disobedience that much more serious. By disobeying God's law and imitating the sins of their idolatrous neighbors, the Jews were sinning against a flood of light. In the covenant, God warned that repeated rebellion would lead to captivity (Lev. 26:27-45; Deut. 28:49-68). The other disciplines took away from the Jews the blessings of the land, but captivity took them away from the land itself. The Jewish people did experience defeat and captivity. Assyria conquered the northern kingdom of Israel in 722 and Babylon conquered the southern kingdom of Judah in 606–586 and took the Jews captive to Babylon. This terrible event was predicted by Isaiah (6:11-12; 11:11-12; 39:6) and Micah (4:10), and Jeremiah revealed that the Babylonian captivity would last for seventy years (Jer. 25:1-14; 29:11-14). When the prophet Daniel understood what Jeremiah wrote, he began to pray that God would keep His promises (Deut. 30:1-10) and set the nation free (Dan.

9:1ff). No doubt many other believing Jews ("the remnant") also interceded, and God stirred Cyrus, king of Persia, to allow the Jews to return to their land and rebuild their temple (Ezra 1; 2 Chron. 36:22-23).

Solomon gave the Lord several reasons why the Lord should forgive His people when they repented and returned to Him. After all, they were His people whom He had purchased and delivered from Egyptian bondage (v. 51). Israel was His special people, separated from the other nations to glorify God and accomplish His mission on earth. Again, Solomon revealed his knowledge of the Book of Deuteronomy (4:20; 7:6; 9:26-29; 32:9).

He closed his prayer by asking the Lord to keep His eyes upon the temple and the people who worshiped there, and to keep His ears open to the requests of the people who prayed at the temple or toward the temple (2 Chron. 6:40-42). His benediction in verse 41 is found in Psalms 132:8-10.[5] Israel was no longer a pilgrim people, but they still needed the Lord to guide and help them. (See also the words of Moses in Num. 10:35-36.) Thanks to David's victories on the battlefield, God had kept His promise and given Israel rest; but as Andrew Bonar said, "Let us be as watchful after the victory as before the battle." Solomon closed the prayer with a plea that the Lord not reject him, the anointed king, David's son and heir. "Remember the mercies of your servant David" (2 Chron. 6:42, NKJV), referring to God's promises to David in the covenant (2 Sam. 7; Ps. 89:19-29).

These "sure mercies of David" (Isa. 55:3, NKJV) involve the coming of Jesus Christ, the Son of David, to be the Savior of the world (Acts 13:32-40).

4. A house of praise (1 Kings 8:54-61; 2 Chron. 7:1-3)
The king had been kneeling on the special platform near the altar, his hands lifted to God, but now he stood to give the people a blessing from the Lord. Usually it was the priests who blessed the people (Num. 6:22-27), but on a special occasion such as this, the king could give the blessing as David did (2 Sam.

6:18, 20). Solomon blessed the whole assembly and through them the entire nation, and he gave thanks to God for His great mercies.

As Solomon reviewed the history of the Jewish nation, his conclusion was that the promises of God had never failed, not even once. God's people had often failed the Lord, but He had never failed them. He promised Moses that He would give the nation rest, and He did (Ex. 33:14). By His power, He enabled Joshua to overcome the nations in Canaan and claim the land for Israel's inheritance. Moses told the people that when they had entered into the promised rest, God would give them a central sanctuary where they could offer their sacrifices and worship God (Deut. 12:1-14); and now that temple had been provided. In his farewell speech to the leaders, Joshua emphasized the same truth (Josh. 23:14-15, and see 21:45). But Joshua also reminded them that the warnings would be fulfilled as well as the promises, and he cautioned them to obey the Lord in all things.

Solomon especially emphasized one promise that God gave to the patriarchs and repeated often in Jewish history, that the Lord would not leave His people or forsake them. God was with Abraham during his life, and He promised to be with Isaac (Gen. 26:3, 24) and Jacob (Gen. 28:15; 31:3; 46:1-4). He renewed this promise to Moses (Ex. 3:12; 33:14), and Moses repeated it to Joshua (Deut. 31:6-8, 17). The Lord Himself also gave the promise to Joshua (Josh. 1:5, 9; 3:7; see 6:27). He also gave it to Gideon (Jud. 6:15-16), and the prophet Samuel repeated it to the nation (1 Sam. 12:22). David encouraged Solomon with this promise when he appointed him to build the temple (1 Chron. 28:20).

After the days of Solomon, the Prophet Isaiah repeated this promise and gave comfort to the Jewish people who would experience the Babylonian captivity (Isa. 41:10, 17; 42:16; 44:21; 49:14-16). The Lord used it to encourage Jeremiah (Jer. 1:8, 19; 20:11), and Jesus gave it to His disciples before He ascended to the Father (Matt. 28:19-20). The church today can claim the promise just as did believers long ago (Heb. 13:5). See also Psalms 27:9; 37:25, 28; 38:21.

Solomon also asked God to help him and his people to have hearts that were inclined to the Lord and eager to obey His commandments (v. 58). He knew the Book of Deuteronomy and must have had 5:29 in mind—"Oh, that they had such a heart in them that they would fear Me and always keep all My commandments, that it might be well with them and with their children forever!" (NKJV). Solomon admonished the people to have sincere hearts and to follow the Lord wholeheartedly (v. 61).

Finally, Solomon asked the Lord to remember the prayer that he had spoken with his lips and from his heart (vv. 59-60). Our spoken words are but breath and sound, and they vanish almost immediately. It encourages us to know that no believing prayer spoken to the Lord is ever forgotten, for God remembers our prayers and answers them in His time and in His own way. (See Rev. 5:8 and 8:3.) Solomon's prayer was not selfish. He wanted the people of Israel to be faithful to the Lord so that all the nations of the earth might come to know and trust the God of Israel. How encouraging to know that the prayer of one man could touch and influence a whole world! God still wants His house to be called "a house of prayer for all nations."

The Lord answered Solomon's request by sending fire from heaven to consume the sacrifices on the altar, and once again the glory of God filled the house (2 Chron. 7:1-3). God sent fire from heaven when Aaron the priest blessed the people (Lev. 9:23-24), and also when Elijah the prophet called upon God (1 Kings 18:38). Now he sent fire when Solomon a king offered his prayer and his sacrifices to the Lord. But the people all responded by bowing to the ground and praising the Lord. Imagine the sound of thousands of people shouting, "Truly He is good, truly His lovingkindness is everlasting" (2 Chron. 7:3, NASB). God had accepted the prayer of the king and the worship of the people!

5. A house of fellowship (1 Kings 8:62-66; 2 Chron. 7:4-10)

The assembly that gathered for the dedication of the temple came from the southernmost boundary of the kingdom ("the river of Egypt" = the Wadi of Egypt) to the northernmost boundary ("the entrance to Hamath") and formed a "great congregation" (v. 65, NKJV; and see 4:21). Many of them brought sacrifices to the Lord and Solomon himself provided 22,000 cattle and 120,000 sheep and goats. The new altar was too small for the offering of so many animals, so to expedite matters, the king sanctified the courtyard and it was used for sacrifices.

It was customary to feast and rejoice during the week set aside for the Feast of Tabernacles. The feast celebrated God's gracious care of His people during their years in the wilderness, and the people of Israel could look back and give thanks. But now they could look around and give thanks for the new temple, the promises of God, and the presence of the glory of the Lord. Just like the other sacrifices, the peace offering (or fellowship offering, Lev. 3 and 7:11-34) was presented to the Lord, but part of the meat was given to the priests and part was retained by the worshiper. He and his family could enjoy a feast and even invite friends to share it with them. The Jews raised their animals for milk, wool, and young and didn't often eat meat, so the fellowship feast after the sacrifice was a real treat. The dedication lasted a week, the feast lasted another week, and the event closed with a day of solemn assembly (2 Chron. 7:8-9). The sacrifices must have been offered day after day, for the meat of the fellowship offering could be eaten only two days and all leftovers had to be burned the third day (Lev. 19:5-8).

While some churches go overboard on eating—"the Upper Room has become the supper room"—there is nothing wrong with God's people eating together. Jesus often used meal settings to teach the Word, and the early church occasionally held what was called "a love feast" (*agape*), a potluck meal that may have been the only decent meal some of the members had all weak, especially the slaves (1 Cor. 11:20-22, 33-34; Jude 12). The members of the various Jerusalem assemblies often ate together (Acts 2:42-47; 4:35; 6:1), and hospitality was a virtue often encouraged in the epistles (Rom. 12:13; 16:23; 1 Tim. 3:2; 5:10; Titus 1:8; 1 Peter 4:9; 3 John 8). "Therefore, whether you eat or drink, or whatever you do, do all to the glory of God" (1 Cor. 10:31, NKJV).

However, the peace offering symbolizes Jesus Christ who is our peace (Eph. 2:14) and who has given us the gift of His peace (John 14:27). Because of His sacrifice on the cross, we have "peace with God" (Rom. 5:1), and by surrendering to Him, we can have "the peace of God" in our hearts (Phil. 4:6-9). God's people "feed" on Jesus Christ as we read the Word and make it a part of our lives, and as we obey what it commands. Jesus Christ is the center of our fellowship, just as at the dedication of the temple the peace offerings were the center of the fellowship.

God doesn't live in the church buildings we erect, but when we assemble in these building dedicated to Him, we ought to emphasize worship, fellowship, joy, and witness. Such meetings are occasions for both joy and solemnity. "Serve the Lord with fear, and rejoice with trembling" (Ps. 2:11, NKJV). When the Holy Spirit is in control, both rejoicing and reverence will characterize the gathering.

6. A house of responsibility (1 Kings 9:1-9; 2 Chron. 7:11-22)
The presence of God's glory in the temple and the coming of fire from heaven to consume the sacrifices assured Solomon that his prayer had been heard and was accepted by the Lord. But there would not always be that same splendor of glory in the temple, nor would fire from heaven consume every sacrifice; so the Lord spoke His Word to Solomon, for "the Word of the Lord endures forever" (1 Peter 1:25).

Promise (vv. 1-3; 2 Chron. 7:11-16). As He had done at Gibeon (3:4-5), the Lord appeared to Solomon and spoke the Word that he needed to hear. He assured the king that He had heard his prayer and would answer it. His eyes would be on the house Solomon had built and dedicated, and His ears would be alert to hear the prayers of His people. The people and their king had dedicated the house to the Lord, but now He would sanctify the house and make it His own. God's name was on the house, God's eyes were watching, and His ears listening. It was indeed the house of the Lord.

The text in 2 Chronicles 7:11-16 mentions some of the specific requests that Solomon had made in his prayer, and the Lord promised to answer every request. He was willing to forgive His people when they sinned if only they would humble themselves, pray, seek His face, and turn from their sins. God has never made a covenant with any other nation but Israel, but since Christian believers today are God's people and called by His name, they can claim this promise.

Obedience (vv. 4-5; 2 Chron. 7:17-18). But the Lord made the matter very personal and spoke specifically to Solomon, referring to the covenant God had made with his father David (2 Sam. 7). The Lord reaffirmed the terms of the covenant and assured Solomon that David would always have a king on the throne so long as his descendants obeyed the law and walked in the fear of the Lord. Solomon couldn't expect God's blessing just because David was his father and he had obeyed David and built the temple. Solomon had to be a man like his father, a man after God's own heart (1 Sam. 13:14), a man of integrity (Ps. 78:72). It's interesting that the Lord said nothing about David's adultery, deception, and plot to murder Uriah. These had been serious transgressions for which David had paid dearly, but David had confessed them and the Lord had forgiven him.

Warning (vv. 6-9; 2 Chron. 7:19-22). God had given the Jewish people His Word, and He expected them to obey it, and the king had to practice the law and set the example for others. It's tragic that after the death of Solomon the nation divided and both kingdoms gradually declined until they were destroyed. The Lord in these words was only rehearsing the terms of the covenant found in Leviticus 26 and Deuteronomy 28-30, a covenant that the Jewish people knew well. The kingdom of Judah did turn to idols, disobey the Lord, and invite His chastening. The Babylonian army devastated the land, destroyed Jerusalem, and robbed and burned the temple Solomon had dedicated. Instead of being a blessing to all the nations of the earth, the ruined city and temple would shock visitors from other nations and move them to ridicule.

Before we pass judgment on David's royal line, let's consider how many local churches, schools, denominational agencies, and other Christian ministries have abandoned the true faith and ceased to bring glory to the Lord. We could honestly write "Ichabod—the glory has departed" on many an edifice in which Christ was once honored and from which the gospel of Jesus Christ was sent out to a lost world.

From Solomon's death in 931 until the reign of Zedekiah (597–586), the Davidic dynasty would continue for God would keep His promise to David. But the only Jew alive today who qualifies to sit on David's throne *and can prove it from the genealogies*, is Jesus of Nazareth, Son of David, Son of God. One day He will reign from David's throne and "the earth will be filled with the knowledge of the glory of the Lord, as the waters cover the sea" (Hab. 2:14, NKJV).

FIVE

The Kingdom, Power, and Glory

Most people remember King Solomon as the man who built the temple of God in Jerusalem, but during his reign, he was occupied with many different activities. These chapters record a series of vignettes depicting some of the things Solomon did to advance his kingdom and enhance his life. But these activities also reveal Solomon's character and expose some of the areas of weakness that later produced a bitter harvest. Gradually, Solomon became more interested in prices than in values, and in reputation rather than character, and in the splendor of the kingdom rather than the good of the people and the glory of the Lord.

1. Solomon builds a palace (1 Kings 7:1-12)

The work on the temple structure was completed in seven years,[1] but it took several more years for Hiram and his crew to decorate the interior and construct the furnishings. While they were busy at the temple, Solomon designed and built a palace for himself that was a combination of personal residence, city hall, armory, and official reception center. "I enlarged my works," he wrote, "I built houses for myself" (Ecc. 2:4, NASB).

When you read this description of the project, you get the

impression that it involved several isolated structures, but 1 Kings 9:10 refers to "the two houses [buildings]," the temple and the "palace." The palace was twice as large as the temple and probably had two if not three stories. It was 150 feet long, 75 feet wide, and 45 feet high. (The temple was 90 x 30 x 45.) The total structure included two porches or colonnades, Solomon's own residence, a residence for his Egyptian wife[2] (and perhaps part of his harem), a throne room ("hall of justice"), and a spacious reception hall, all tied together by a large courtyard set off by walls like those at the temple.

We don't have a detailed description to guide us, but it appears that when you approached the building, you came to a smaller porch that served as the main entrance (v. 7). This led to a larger porch or colonnade with cedar pillars, which probably served as a waiting room. From here you moved into "the hall of pillars," a large assembly hall with sixty cedar pillars (vv. 2-3), forty-five of which held up the cedar-beamed ceiling that formed the floor of the second story. Fifteen pillars were placed opposite each other against the side walls, to the right and left of the entrance, and fifteen down the center of the room, all bearing the cedar beams. The other fifteen pillars were placed strategically where needed, especially at the entrance (see v. 6, NIV).

Because of the abundance of these cedar pillars from Lebanon, the structure was known as "the Palace of the Forest of Lebanon." The assembly hall was no doubt used for official government occasions. In this hall, Solomon displayed three hundred large shields and two hundred smaller shields, all made of wood covered with gold (10:16-17). The larger ones used seven and a half pounds of gold each, a total of 1,500 pounds, and the smaller shields three-and a half pounds apiece, making 1,025 pounds, a total of 2,525 pounds of gold for all five hundred shields. Since gold is too soft to provide protection, these shields were not used in battle but were there to impress visitors. They were taken from the building only when displayed on special ceremonial occasions.

From the hall you moved into the throne room, the "Hall of Justice," where Solomon met with his officers, settled disputes referred to him, and gave judgment concerning governmental affairs. It was there he had his magnificent throne described in 10:18-20. Solomon's living quarters, and, we assume, the queen's quarters, were behind this throne room (7:7-8 NIV). Of course there were other entrances to various parts of the building, all of them protected by the king's special bodyguard, and Solomon had a private concourse that led from his residence to the temple. Next to the temple of the Lord, Solomon's "palace" must have been an imposing structure.

2. Solomon disappoints a friend (1 Kings 9:10-14; 2 Chron. 8:1-2)
Hiram, king of Tyre, had been David's good friend, and David had told him about his plans to build a temple for the Lord (5:1-3), plans the Lord didn't permit David to carry out. After David's death, Solomon became Hiram's friend (Prov. 27:10) and contracted with Hiram to help build the temple (5:1-12). Hiram would send timber and workers if Solomon would pay the workers and provide Hiram with food in return for the timber. Solomon also conscripted Jewish men to cut stone (5:13-18) and the aliens in the land to help bear burdens (9:15, 20-23; 2 Chron. 8:7-10).

But 1 Kings 9:11 and 14 inform us that Hiram also supplied Solomon with 120 talents of gold (about four and a half tons)! King Solomon had at least 3,750 tons of gold available before he began to build the temple (1 Chron. 22:14-16), and the fact that he had to get gold from Hiram surprises us. The gold, silver, and other materials for the temple that are inventoried in 1 Chronicles 22, 28–29 were all dedicated to the Lord, so they couldn't be used for any other building. This means Solomon needed the gold for the "palace" complex, perhaps for the gold shields, so he borrowed it from Hiram, giving him the twenty cities as collateral. These cities were conveniently located on the border of Phoenicia and Galilee.[3]

Apart from the fact that Solomon shouldn't have been so extravagant in building his "palace," he didn't have the right to give twenty cities away just to pay his debts. All the land belonged to the Lord and could not be deeded away permanently (Lev. 25:23). One purpose for the Year of Jubilee (Lev. 25:8ff) was to make sure the land that had been sold was returned to the original owners and so that no clan or tribe could be deprived of their inheritance. But Solomon was starting to behave like his Egyptian father-in-law who had wiped out the population of an entire Canaanite city and given the city to his daughter as a wedding gift (v. 16).

But Hiram didn't like the cities that Solomon gave him! After looking them over, he called them "Cabul" which sounds like a Hebrew word that means "good for nothing." He didn't think the collateral was worth the investment he had made. However, the story seems to have had a happy ending. Solomon must have paid back the loan because Hiram returned the cities to him and Solomon rebuilt them for the Israelites (2 Chron. 8:1-2). Did Solomon pay off the loan with the 120 talents of gold that the Queen of Sheba gave him (10:10)?

Solomon exhibits in this incident some character traits that disturb us, including the extravagant cost of the "palace" that necessitated a loan, and then giving a friend poor collateral that wasn't even his to give away. Humanly speaking, were it not for Hiram, the temple would not have been built, and this was no way for Solomon to treat a generous friend.

3. Solomon strengthens his kingdom (1 Kings 9:15-24; 2 Chron. 8:1-11)

When the Lord appeared to Solomon in Gibeon, He promised to give him riches and honor to such an extent that there would be no king like him all the days of his life (3:13). He kept that promise and made Solomon's name famous and his accomplishments admired by people in other nations. Solomon's father David had conquered enemy territory and added it to the kingdom, but he hadn't attempted to build an international network that would make Israel powerful among the nations. David was a mighty general who feared no enemy, but Solomon was a shrewd diplomat and politician who missed no opportunity to increase his wealth and power. This section lists for us the achievements of Solomon both at home and abroad.

We don't usually think of Solomon as being a military man, but this one exploit is recorded in Scripture (2 Chron. 8:3). Hamath was a city north of Damascus at the farthest northern border of the kingdom of Israel (Num. 34:8; Josh. 13:5). People from this area attended the dedication of the temple (8:65; 2 Chron. 7:8). The city was situated on a very important trade route from which Solomon could collect custom and duty and also guard against invaders. Along with Hamath, Solomon fortified Hazor, Megiddo, and Gezer and made them "store cities," that is, places where chariots, horses, arms, and food were stored for the use of the Jewish troops. Solomon knew that if he didn't protect the outlying areas of the kingdom, he might find himself at war with his neighbors, his treaties notwithstanding.

Solomon also strengthened and extended "the Millo," the terraced area next to the walls of Jerusalem that buttressed the wall and gave more protection to the city. The word *millo* means "to fill." This was an "earth-fill fortification" that was begun by David (2 Sam. 5:9) and continued by Solomon (9:24; 11:27). The king and his family, the people of the city, and the wealth in the temple and the palace all had to be protected.

To accomplish all this work, the king conscripted the aliens in Israel, the descendants of the Canaanites who had once ruled the land (v. 20; Gen. 15:18-21; Josh. 3:10). In building the temple, he had also enlisted the temporary help of the Jewish men (5:13-14; 9:15, 22-23), but no Jewish worker was treated like a slave. The Jews were made officers and leaders in these building projects.

4. Solomon worships the Lord (1 Kings 9:25; 2 Chron. 8:12-16)
Annually, the adult Jewish males in Israel were required to appear at Jerusalem to celebrate Passover, Pentecost, and Tabernacles, (Ex. 23:14-19; Deut. 16:1-17). To Christian believers today, these three feasts signify the death of Christ, the Lamb of God, for our sins (John 1:29; 1 Cor. 5:7); the resurrection of Christ and the coming of the Holy Spirit (1 Cor. 15:23; Acts 2);

and the future regathering of God's people in the kingdom (Rev. 20:1-6). To the Jewish people, Passover looked back to their deliverance from Egyptian bondage while Tabernacles commemorated God's care during their years in the wilderness. Firstfruits celebrated the goodness of God in sending the harvest.

Solomon lived in Jerusalem, but he set an example by going to the temple and offering sacrifices. Of course, it was the priests who offered both the sacrifices and the incense. The burnt offering signified total dedication to the Lord; the fellowship or peace offerings spoke of peace with God and communion with Him and one another; and the burning incense was a picture of prayer offered to the Lord (Ex. 30:1-10; Ps. 141:2; Rev. 8:3). There are no instances in Scripture of the common people bringing incense to be offered on the golden altar, since this was a task the priests performed twice daily for the whole nation. However, Psalm 72, "A Psalm for Solomon," mentions continual prayer to be made for the king (v. 15), and there is no reason why Solomon could not have provided some of the spices needed for the special incense (10:2, 10; Ex. 30:34-38).

The account in 2 Chronicles 8 indicates that Solomon also provided the sacrifices that were needed during these feasts as well as on the special Sabbaths and the new moon festivals. He obeyed the Law of Moses in this regard, and he also followed the plan instituted by his father David for the ministry of the priests and Levites in the temple (1 Chron. 23–26). Asaph was chief over the musicians (1 Chron. 16:4-5), and there were 4,000 singers divided into twenty-four courses. Each singer ministered at the temple two weeks every year. There was also a special choir of 288 singers (1 Chron. 25:7). Solomon was careful to see to it that David's songs and instruments were used and that his plan for organizing the priests and Levites was honored.

5. Solomon expands his influence (1 Kings 8:26–10:13; 2 Chron. 8:17-9:12)

Solomon was a great entrepreneur. He made trade agreements with many nations, built a navy, and hired Hiram's expert seamen to manage it for him. Being an inland people for the most part, the Jews were not given to maritime pursuits, so Solomon depended on the Phoenicians, a coastal people, to handle this aspect of his enterprises. Importing products from the east enriched Solomon's coffers and helped to make the kingdom more international in its outlook. This outreach surely gave opportunities for the Jews to bear witness of their God to the pagan Gentiles, but there's no record that there was such a ministry. Solomon had to maintain a huge budget and he needed as much money as he could get. On one trip they brought back 420 talents of gold, about sixteen tons of gold. The ships also brought luxury items like ivory, apes, and peacocks. It appears that Solomon also had a zoo (Ecc. 2:4-9). The words of the English poet Oliver Goldsmith come to mind –

> Ill fares the land, to hast'ning ills a prey,
> Where wealth accumulates, and men decay . . .[4]

The visit of the queen of Sheba (10:1-13) was undoubtedly motivated both by Solomon's mercantile endeavors as well as her own desires to meet Solomon, see the glories of his kingdom, and test his highly esteemed wisdom. Sheba was a wealthy and highly civilized nation located in southwest Arabia, and the queen brought with her expensive gifts that also served as samples of what her country had to offer (Isa. 60:6; Jer. 6:20; Ezek. 38:13). She "told him all her heart" and he told her what she wanted to know. What she heard and what she saw left her breathless. She had heard the reports but she didn't really believe them until she saw it all for herself. We're reminded of the experience of Thomas (John 20:24-29).

But the record of her visit gives us opportunity to get a glimpse of life in the palace. The queen not only marveled at Solomon's palace, but she was impressed by the meals (4:7, 22-23), the livery and conduct of the servants, the seating of the officers and guests, and the incredible wealth that was displayed on and around the tables. She walked with Solomon on his private concourse to the temple where she watched him worship. (See 10:5 and 2 Chron. 9:4, NIV margin.) The wisdom of Solomon's words and the wealth of Solomon's kingdom were just too much for her, and she was no pauper herself! She brought Solomon expensive gifts, including an abundance of spices and 120 talents of gold (four and a half tons). Solomon reciprocated by giving her whatever she asked for out of his royal bounty.

The queen couldn't contain herself. She announced publicly that Solomon and his servants had to be the happiest people on earth, yet it was Solomon who later wrote the Book of Ecclesiastes and declared, "Vanity of vanities, all is vanity!" We wonder if Solomon's officers and servants didn't gradually grow accustomed to all the pomp and circumstance of court life, especially the gaudy display of wealth. Even Solomon wrote, "Better is a little with the fear of the Lord, than great treasure with trouble. Better is a dinner of herbs [vegetables] where love is, than a fatted calf with hatred" (Prov. 15:16-17, NKJV). Hearing Solomon's words of wisdom may have excited the dinner guests, but the officers and servants had heard it before. One of the dangers of living in that kind of situation is that we begin to take things for granted, and before long, we don't value them at all. This can apply to spiritual treasures as well as material wealth.

When the queen said, "Blessed be the Lord, your God," she wasn't affirming her personal faith in Jehovah. People in those days believed in "territorial deities." Each nation had its own god or gods (1 Kings 20:28) and when you left your land, you left your gods behind (1 Sam. 26:19). Once she returned home, the queen would worship the gods of her own land, even though she had seen the glories of the God of Israel and heard His wisdom. Jesus didn't commend the queen of Sheba for her faith but for the fact that she made every effort to travel about 1,500 miles to hear the wisdom of Solomon, when the Son of God, one "greater than Solomon," was in the midst of the Jewish people (Matt. 12:39-42). The tragedy of lost opportunity!

It's interesting to contrast this account of the meeting of Solomon and the queen of Sheba with the account of Solomon's first act of justice as king when he met two prostitutes (3:16ff). They were commoners but she was a queen, and they had very little but she was very wealthy. Yet the king's door was open to all three of these women and he sought to help them. Of course, the queen of Sheba negotiated a trade pact with Solomon, but there's no evidence that she trusted the true and living God.

The commercial network that Solomon established certainly helped the economy of the nation and brought many influential visitors to Jerusalem, but did it help the king and his people draw near to God? Israel wasn't supposed to be isolated from the community of nations, because she was to be a light to the Gentiles, but she was supposed to be separated from the sins of those nations that didn't know the true and living God. Along with the influx of foreign merchandise came the influx of foreign ideas, including ideas about religion and worship; and eventually Solomon himself, influenced by his foreign wives, succumbed to idolatry (11:1ff).

6. Solomon lives in splendor (1 Kings 10:14-29; 2 Chron. 9:13-28)
When God promised to give Solomon wisdom, He also promised him riches and honor (3:13). It isn't a sin to possess wealth or to inherit wealth. Abraham was a very wealthy man who gave all his wealth to his son Isaac (Gen. 24:34-36). Earning money honestly isn't a sin, but loving money and living just to acquire riches is a sin (1 Tim. 6:7-10).

Solomon himself wrote, "Whoever loves money never has money enough; whoever loves wealth is never satisfied with his income. This too is meaningless" (Ecc. 5:10, NIV). Someone has wisely said, "It's good to have the things that money can buy, provided you don't lose the things money can't buy."

Solomon's annual income was 666 talents of gold, or about twenty-five tons.[5] It came from several sources: (1) taxes, (2) tolls, customs, and duty fees, (3) trade, (4) tribute from vassal rulers, and (5) gifts. His use of conscripted labor was also a form of income. It took a great deal of money to support his splendid manner of life, and after Solomon's death, the people of Israel protested the yoke they were wearing and asked for the burden to be lightened (12:1-15).

Why did Solomon need five hundred shields that required 2,525 pounds of gold to make? Why did he need an ivory throne overlaid with gold? Why must he and his guests drink only from golden vessels? To what purpose were the thousands of horses and chariots he assembled? Why did he need seven hundred wives and three hundred concubines? *In pursuing each of these goals, Solomon disobeyed the very Word of the Lord!* The Lord warned in Deuteronomy 17:14-20 that Israel's king was not to multiply horses and go to Egypt to get them, nor was he to multiply wives or gold. Solomon not only acquired thousands of horses, but he became a horse dealer himself! Deuteronomy 17:20 warns the king that he must remain humble before the Lord "and not consider himself better than his brothers." It's not difficult to believe that Solomon's heart was lifted up with pride, and pride always leads to destruction and a fall (Prov. 16:18).

To the world of that day, and especially to the Jewish people, Solomon became a model of wealth and splendor, and no doubt many envied him. But Jesus said that one of the Father's lilies was more beautifully arrayed than Solomon in all his glory (Matt. 6:28-30). True beauty comes from within, from "the hidden person of the heart" (1 Peter 3:4, NKJV). The more we must add to our possessions before people will admire us, the less true wealth and beauty we really have.

David had prophets and priests who advised him and even warned and rebuked him, but nobody seems to have admonished Solomon to pay more attention to making a life instead of amassing a fortune. A Roman proverb says, "Riches are like salt water—the more you drink, the more you thirst." Henry David Thoreau said that a man is rich in proportion to the number of things he can afford to do without; and Jesus asked, "For what profit is it to a man if he gains the whole world, and loses his own soul?" (Matt. 16:26, NKJV).

1 KINGS 11:1-43
[2 CHRONICLES 9:29-31]

The Foolish Wise Man

"Scripture never blinks the defects of its heroes," wrote the gift-ed British expositor Alexander Maclaren. "Its portraits do not smooth out wrinkles, but, with absolute fidelity, give all faults."[1] This inspired biblical honesty is seen in the record of the life of King Solomon. God gave Solomon unusual wisdom, incredible wealth, and great opportunities, but in his older years, he turned from the Lord, made foolish decisions, and didn't end well. "A man's own folly ruins his life" (Prov. 19:3, NIV). Solomon wrote those words and probably believed them, but he didn't heed them.

It isn't difficult to trace the steps in Solomon's downward path.

1. Solomon disobeyed God's Word (1 Kings 11:1-8)
Going back to Egypt may have been Solomon's first step in turn-ing away from the Lord. He secured a bride from Egypt (v. 1; 3:1; 9:24) and he purchased horses and chariots there (4:26-28; 10:26-29). Both of these actions revealed Solomon's unbelief. He mar-ried the Egyptian princess in order to establish a peace treaty with her father, and he wanted horses and chariots because he didn't really believe that Jehovah could protect the land. What his father

David had written was not in Solomon's creed: "Some trust in chariots, and some in horses; but we will remember the name of the Lord our God" (Ps. 20:7, NKJV). His marriages and his procuring of horses and chariots were in direct disobedience to the Lord's clear commands (Deut. 17:16; 7:1-6; Ex., 23:31-34; 34:15-16; Josh. 23:12-13). Solomon's bad example in choosing wives from pagan nations created problems for Ezra and Nehemiah over four centuries later (Ezra 9:2; 10:2-3; Neh. 13:23-27).

In terms of "biblical geography," Egypt represents the bondage of the world.[2] The wilderness pictures the unbelief of God's people today as, like Israel, they wander and fail to lay hold of their inheritance in Christ.[3] The Promised Land represents the rest God gives to those who trust Christ, submit to Him, and go forth to conquer by faith. All believers have been delivered from the world system that is contrary to God (Gal. 1:4), and all believers are exhorted to claim their inheritance in Christ now and not to wander aimlessly through life. No Christian believer has to trust the world for anything, because we have received in Christ every blessing that we need (Eph. 1:3; 2 Peter 1:1-4). We are in the world physically but not of the world spiritually (John 17:14:19), and all our needs come to us from the Father in heaven (Matt. 6:11; Phil. 4:19).

The danger of marrying pagan unbelievers is spelled out in v. 2, NKJV, which is a quotation from Deuteronomy 7:4: "they will turn away your heart after their gods." That's exactly what happened to Solomon (vv. 3, 4, 9). The Ammonites and Moabites were descendants of Abraham's nephew Lot (Gen. 19:30ff). The Ammonites worshiped the hideous god Molech and sacrificed their infants on his altars (Lev. 18:21; 20:1-5; and see Jer. 7:29-34; Ezek. 16:20-22). Chemosh was the chief god of the Moabites, and Ashtereth (Astarte) was the goddess of the people of Tyre and Sidon. As the goddess of fertility, her worship included "legalized prostitution" involving both male and female temple prostitutes, and that worship was unspeakably filthy. (See Deut. 23:1-8; 1 Kings 14:24; 15:12; 22:46.) The Babylonians also worshiped this goddess and called her Ishtar.

Solomon had exhorted the people to have hearts that were "perfect with the Lord" (8:61, KJV), that is, undivided and totally yielded to Him alone; yet his own heart wasn't perfect with God (v. 4). Solomon didn't totally abandon Jehovah but made Him one of the many gods that he worshiped (9:25). This was a direct violation of the first two commandments given at Sinai (Ex. 20:1-6). The Lord Jehovah is the only God, the true and living God, and He will not be put on the same level as the false idols of the nations. "For I am God, and there is no other; I am God, and there is none like Me" (Isa. 46:9, NKJV).

Solomon's compromise wasn't a sudden thing, for he gradually descended into his idolatry (Ps. 1:1). First he permitted his wives to worship their own gods; then he tolerated their idolatry and even built shrines for them. Eventually he began to participate in pagan practices with his wives. His sensual love for his many wives was more compelling than his spiritual love for the Lord, the God of Israel. He was a man with a divided and disobedient heart, and people who are double-minded and unstable are dangerous (James 1:8). How could Israel be a light to the Gentiles nations when their king was openly worshiping and supporting the idols of those nations? He used to offer sacrifices and burn incense only to the Lord Jehovah, but when he got older, he started to include the false gods his wives worshiped (8:25; 11:8).

When you read the Book of Ecclesiastes, you discover that when Solomon's heart began to turn from the Lord, he went through a period of cynicism and despair. He even questioned whether his life was worth living. Without a close walk with the Lord, his heart was empty, so he pursued pleasure, became involved in commercial ventures with many foreign nations, and engaged in vast building programs. However, he still found no enjoyment in life. At least thirty-eight times in Ecclesiastes, Solomon wrote, "Vanity of vanities."

His love for spiritual values was replaced by a love for physical pleasures and material wealth, and gradually his heart turned from the Lord. First he was friendly with the world (James 4:4), then spotted by the world (James 1:27), and then he came to love the world (1 John 2:15-17) and be conformed to the world (Rom. 12:2). Unfortunately, the result of this decline can lead to being condemned with the world and losing everything (1 Cor. 11:32). That's what happened to Lot (Gen. 13:10-13; 14:11-12; 19:1ff), and it can happen to believers today.

2. Solomon ignored God's warning (1 Kings 11:9-13)
The Lord wasn't impressed with Solomon's royal splendor, for the Lord looks on the heart (1 Sam. 16:7) and searches the heart (1 Chron. 28:9; Jer. 17:10; Rev. 2:23). It was Solomon who wrote, "Keep your heart with all diligence, for out of it spring the issues of life" (Prov. 4:23, NKJV), yet in his old age, his own heart was far from the Lord. Since the discovery of the circulation of the blood by William Harvey in the 17th century, everybody knows that the center of human physical life is the heart. But what's true physically is also true morally and spiritually. We're to love God with all our heart (Deut. 6:5) and receive His Word into our hearts (Prov. 7:1-3). God wants us to do His will from our hearts (Eph. 6:6). If our heart is wrong toward God, our entire life will be wrong, no matter how successful we may appear to others.

When Solomon was born, he was greatly loved by the Lord and given the special name "Jedidiah" which means "beloved of the Lord (2 Sam. 12:24-25). But now we read that God was angry with Solomon because the king's heart had turned from the Lord. Solomon was turning his back on a wealth of blessing God had given to him and sinning against a flood of light. To begin with, the Lord had given Solomon a father who, though he wasn't per-fect (and who is?), was devoted to the Lord with a single heart. David had prayed for Solomon and encouraged him to do the will of God and build the temple. Twice the Lord had appeared to Solomon (3:5; 9:2) and reminded him of the terms of the covenant He had made with his father (2 Sam. 7). Solomon cer-tainly knew the terms of the covenant in Deuteronomy 28–30, for he referred to them in his prayer when he dedicated the temple.

We don't know how God delivered this warning to Solomon; perhaps it was through a prophet. But God warned Solomon that, after his death, the kingdom would be divided and his son would reign over only the tribes of Judah and Benjamin. The other ten tribes would become the northern kingdom of Israel. The verb "tear" in verse 11 is picked up in the "action sermon" of Ahijah the prophet when he tore Jeroboam's new robe into twelve parts (vv. 29ff). This division of the kingdom wouldn't be the peaceful work of a diplomat but the painful work of angry Lord.

Were it not for God's covenant with David and His love for Jerusalem, the city where His temple stood, He would have taken the entire kingdom away from Solomon's descendants. God promised David a dynasty that would not end, and therefore He kept one of David's descendants on the throne in Jerusalem until the city was taken by the Babylonians and destroyed. Of course, the ultimate fulfillment of that covenant promise is in Jesus Christ (Luke 1:32-33, 69; Acts 2:29-36; Ps. 89:34-37). God's name was upon the temple (1 Kings 8:43), so He preserved Jerusalem; and God's covenant was with David, so He preserved David's dynasty. Such is the grace of God.

There is no evidence that Solomon took this warning to heart. Had he remembered his own dedication prayer, he could have looked toward the temple and confessed his sins to he Lord.

3. Solomon resisted God's discipline (1 Kings 11:14-25)

Solomon's many marriages had been his guarantees of peace with the neighboring rulers, and Solomon's reign had been a peaceful one. But now his system would start to fall apart, for the Lord raised up "adversaries" against Solomon (vv. 14, 23, 25) and used them to discipline the rebellious king. That God would discipline David's disobedient heirs was a part of the covenant (2 Sam. 7:14-15) and was reaffirmed to Solomon when God spoke to him at Gibeon (3:14). It was repeated while Solomon was building the temple (6:11-13) and after the temple was dedicated (9:3-9). See also 1 Chronicles 22:10 and Psalm 89:30-37. The king certainly could not have been ignorant of the dangers of disobeying the Lord. Three of Solomon's opponents are mentioned specifically.

Hadad the Edomite (vv. 14-22). Solomon had women from Edom in his harem (v. 1), but this didn't stop Hadad from making trouble for Israel. David and Joab had won a great victory over Edom and wiped out the male population (2 Sam. 8:13-14; 1 Chron. 18:11-13; see Ps. 60 title), but Hadad, one of the princes, had fled with some of his father's leaders and found asylum with Pharaoh in Egypt. This must have been a new Pharaoh who didn't find it necessary to recognize Solomon's marriage treaty with the Egyptian princess. Even more, he not only gave Hadad food and a place to live, but he also gave him his own sister-in-law as his wife, and Hadad had a son by her. This meant that Egypt and Edom were now in league against Israel.

The death of King David and his general Joab meant that it was safe for Hadad and his band to return to Edom. There Hadad planned to strengthen the nation and direct a series of attacks against the Israelites. Hadad knew he couldn't take over Solomon's kingdom, but the Lord used him to harass Solomon and his troops in a series of border attacks. This constant irritation from the south should have reminded Solomon that God was disciplining him and calling him back to a life of obedience.

Rezon of Damascus (vv. 23-25). When David defeated the Syrians at Zobah (2 Sam. 8:5-8), a young man named Rezon fled to Damascus with his band of soldiers and set himself up as king. David apparently recognized him as king, and Rezon must have been a capable man because the power of Syria increased under his leadership. But Rezon allied himself with Hadad, leader of Edom, and began to harass Solomon from the north. Rezon established a dynasty of strong rulers in the area (known as Aram), all of whom gave trouble to the kings of Judah (15:18-20; 20:1ff; 2 Kings 8-13 and 15-16 *passim.*) Rezin was king of Aram (Syria) during the time of Isaiah the prophet (Isa. 7:1-8; 8:6; 9:11).

4. Solomon opposed God's servant (1 Kings 11:26-43; 2 Chron. 9:29-31)
Hadad attacked Solomon from the south and Rezon from the

north, but Jeroboam was one of Solomon's own leaders who threatened the king from within the official ranks. He was an Ephraimite who displayed excellent management qualities and caught the eye of the king. Since Jeroboam was from the tribe of Ephraim, Solomon put him in charge of the Jewish labor force from the house of Joseph, namely the tribes of Ephraim and Manasseh. By now, the nation had grown weary of Solomon's building projects and especially of the way he conscripted Jews to do the work (5:13-18), and young Jeroboam had his introduction to the undercurrents of opposition against the king. This knowledge, plus the fact that Solomon had put him over northern tribes, would assist him when the time came to establish the ten northern tribes in their own kingdom.

One day in the course of his own work, Jeroboam was stopped by Ahijah the prophet from Shiloh who had a message for him from God. During Solomon's reign, prophets didn't play a prominent role, but prophets will be very important from now until the end of the kingdom of Judah. Whenever the kings or the priests defied the Word of God, the Lord often sent a prophet to warn them. Prophets were "forth-tellers" more than "fore-tellers." They came with a message from God for that present day, and if they revealed anything about the future, it was to help them call people back to obedience to God's will.[4]

Ahijah dramatized his message by tearing Jeroboam's new garment into twelve parts and giving him ten of them. This was God's way of saying that Jeroboam would become king of the ten northern tribes of Israel.[5] Ahijah explained why two tribes were still reserved for the house of David and also why Solomon's son was being given only those two tribes. Solomon had sinned greatly by introducing idolatry into the land, a sin that would eventually destroy the nation and lead them into captivity.

It was for David's sake that God protected Judah and Jerusalem. Solomon hadn't kept the terms of the covenant God made with his father (2 Sam. 7), but God would be faithful to His Word (2 Sam. 7:11-13). The lamp would burn for David until the end of the Jewish monarchy with the fall of Zedekiah (2

Kings 25; see 1 Kings 11:36; 15:4; 2 Kings 8:19; 21:7; Ps. 132:17).

Ahijah closed his message by warning Jeroboam that what happened to him was wholly of God's grace. He had better take his calling seriously and obey the Word of the Lord, or God would discipline him just as He had to discipline Solomon. God would give Jeroboam an enduring dynasty if he obeyed the law of God. However, that dynasty would not replace the dynasty of David in Judah, for from David's dynasty the Messiah would come and fulfill the covenant promises. God humbled David's successors by giving them only two tribes, but He wouldn't humble them forever. There would be a healing of the division of the nation when Messiah came (Jer. 30:9; Ezek. 34:23; 37:15-28; Hos. 3:5; Amos 9:11-12), and then the king would reign over the whole nation.[6]

Since Ahijah and Jeroboam were alone in the field when the message was delivered (v. 29), we don't know how the word of Jeroboam's special call reached Solomon's ears. Jeroboam may have told some of his close associates who were distressed by the way the king was treating the people, or perhaps God gave Ahijah permission to send the message to Solomon. This message was God's last word of discipline and rebuke for the wayward king, for what more could He do to awaken the king than to take most of the kingdom away from his successor? Solomon should have fallen on his face in repentance and contrition and sought the face of the Lord, but instead he tried to kill his rival. Jeroboam fled to Egypt for safety. The new Pharaoh was Shishak, a man who had no obligations to the house of David.

Solomon had forsaken the Lord (v. 33; see 9:9), and this would be the recurring sin of many kings of Israel and Judah (18:18; 19:10, 14; 2 Kings 17:16; 21:22; 22:17). The sin of idolatry cut at the very heart of Israel's faith, Jehovah was the only true and living God, the God of Abraham, Isaac, and Jacob.

Solomon reigned from 971 to 931. Did he return to the Lord before he died? Bible students don't agree in their interpretations and answers. Certainly his admonition in Ecclesiastes 12:13-14 points in the direction of repentance and restoration, and we trust this was so. The accomplishments of his very full life were recorded not only in 1 Kings and 2 Chronicles, but also in some books that we don't possess, including the Acts of Solomon (possible an official register), a book by Nathan the prophet, as well as records by Ahijah and Iddo. Solomon is the first Jewish king whose death was recorded in the "official words" of verses 41-43 and 2 Chron. 9:29-31. See also 2 Chronicles 9:29; 12:15; 26:22; and 32:32.

Like King Saul, Solomon was handed great opportunities but didn't make the most of them. He knew a great deal about animals, plants, bringing wealth to the nation, and constructing buildings, but he was defective in sharing the knowledge of the Lord[7] with the Gentiles who came to his throne room. Like his father David, Solomon had a gift for enjoying women, but when Solomon sinned, he didn't have David's sincere heart and broken spirit of repentance. The grandeur of the kingdom and not the glory of the Lord was what motivated Solomon's life.

He left behind the temple of God, his royal palace, a nation in bondage, an economy in trouble, as well as the books of Proverbs, Ecclesiastes, and the Song of Solomon. The nation was united during his reign, but there was a hairline split in the nation that eventually revealed itself in open rebellion and division. Solomon's hunger for wealth and achievement put a heavy financial burden on the nation, and after his death, the people revolted.

But the people did worse than that: they followed Solomon's bad example and began to worship the gods of their neighbors. It was this sin more than any other that brought about the downfall of the Jewish nation. "Solomon imported the wives," wrote William Sanford LaSor, "the wives imported the gods; Solomon tolerated it, encouraged it, built places of worship for these idolaters. What can you expect the people to do but follow along?"

May our allegiance always be sincere and loyal to Jesus Christ, the one "greater than Solomon," who died for us, who lives for us and one day will come for us!

SEVEN

1 KINGS 12:1-24; 14:21-31
[2 CHRONICLES 10:1–12:16]

He Would Not Listen

"Then I hated all my labor in which I toiled under the sun," Solomon wrote in Ecclesiastes, "because I must leave it to the man who will come after me. And who knows whether he will be a wise man or a fool?" (Ecc. 2:18-19, NKJV).

His successor was his son Rehoboam, who occasionally made a shrewd decision but for the most part was a foolish ruler. At the beginning of Rehoboam's reign, a selfish decision on his part divided the nation, and during his fourth year, Rehoboam decided to turn from the Lord and worship idols, and that brought the judgment of the Lord. His reign could hardly be called successful.

According to 1 Kings 14:21, Rehoboam was forty-one years old when he began to reign.[1] Since Solomon reigned for forty years (11:42), this means that Rehoboam was born before Solomon became king. But the same text informs us that Rehoboam's mother was an Ammonite woman named Naamah,[2] which means that the Egyptian princess Solomon married was not his first wife (3:1). His father David had married a princess from Geshur, a nation in Syria, and she became the mother of Absalom (2 Sam. 3:3). This was undoubtedly a political move on David's part, so perhaps Solomon's marriage to an Ammonite woman didn't upset David in his latter years. The Hebrew text of 14:21 reads "Naamah *the* Ammonite" (italics mine), suggesting that she was distinguished above the other Ammonite women in the court. This would include Solomon's Ammonite wives and concubines, which Rehoboam inherited when he became king.

What life does to us depends on what life finds in us. During Rehoboam's reign of seventeen years, the way he responded to situations revealed what kind of a person he really was. At least four characteristics stand out in his short reign.

1. An arrogant king (1 Kings 12:1-17; 2 Chron. 10:1-19)

Alexander Maclaren called this account "a miserable story of imbecility and arrogance," and he was right. The story reveals that, whatever gifts Rehoboam may have possessed, he didn't have the gift of relating to people and understanding their needs. David was a king who loved his people and risked his life for their welfare. Solomon was a king who didn't serve the people but used the people to satisfy his own desires. Reheboam was a king who ignored the lessons of the past and turned his ears away from the voices of the suffering people. He was unfit to rule.

The assembly at Shechem (vv. 1-3; 2 Chron. 10:1-3). Solomon must have made it clear that Rehoboam was to be the next king, but it was still necessary for the people to affirm the choice and enter into covenant with God and the king. This had been done when Saul became king (1 Sam. 10:17) and also when David and Solomon were each crowned (2 Sam. 2:4; 5:1ff; 1 Kings 1:28ff). Rehoboam and his officers appointed Shechem as the meeting place, and Jeroboam and the men of the Northern Kingdom attended.[3] Jeroboam had returned from his asylum in Egypt and was the acknowledged leader of the northern ten tribes. Rehoboam knew this man was his enemy, but he didn't dare openly oppose him lest he alienate the people. Surely Rehoboam also knew the prophecy given by Ahijah that Jeroboam would become ruler of the Northern Kingdom, but perhaps he didn't think it would really occur. No doubt he thought that the Davidic dynasty and the Solomonic prosperity would carry the day. He forgot 2 Sam. 7:12-14.

If Rehoboam selected Shechem for this important meeting, it was one of the smartest things he ever did. Shechem was located about forty miles north of Jerusalem, a good central city for such an important meeting. It was situated in the tribe of Manasseh, and this would please the people in the northern ten tribes. Joseph's tomb was at Shechem (Josh. 24:32), the tabernacle had been in Shiloh in Ephraim, and Samuel the prophet was from the hill country of Ephraim (1 Sam. 1:1). Abraham, the father of the Jewish nation, had been in Shechem (Gen. 12:6) and so had Jacob (Gen. 33:18). Joshua had confirmed the covenant with Israel at Shechem (Josh. 24), so Shechem was a place of great historical and spiritual significance to the Jewish people.

Ephraim, and Manasseh, the descendants of Joseph, considered themselves the leading tribes in Israel and openly expressed their resentment of the leadership of Judah (Ps. 78:60, 67). David had welcomed volunteers from Ephraim and Manasseh into his warrior band (1 Chron. 12:30-31); but for years, Ephraim and Manasseh had sown seeds of division and dissention in the land (see Jud. 8:1; 12:1). Perhaps Rehoboam thought that being crowned at Shechem would be a step toward peace and unity between the north and the south, but it turned out to be just the opposite.

The appeal of the ten tribes (vv. 4-5; 2 Chron. 10:4-5). Led by Jeroboam, the leaders of the northern tribes protested the heavy yoke that Rehoboam's father had laid on them, including high taxes and forced labor. When Solomon reorganized the land into twelve districts (4:7-19), it appears that Judah wasn't included, and this policy may have been followed when he conscripted laborers (5:13-18). We can easily understand how the other tribes would respond to such blatant favoritism. Why should these hardworking people sacrifice just so the king could live in a magnificent house, be pampered by servants, and eat daily at a festive table? The people were wearing a galling yoke and they were tired of it.

Back in the days of the judges, when Israel had asked for a

king, Samuel warned them that having a king would be a very costly luxury (1 Sam. 8:10-22). The very things Samuel warned about were done by Solomon and would be continued by Rehoboam unless he altered his policies. It must have irritated Rehoboam that Jeroboam was the spokesman for the ten northern tribes, for surely he knew about the prophecy of Ahijah and that his father Solomon had tried to kill Jeroboam (11:29-40). Furthermore, Jeroboam was a favorite in Egypt and Rehoboam didn't know what plans he and Pharaoh had made together. The kingdom was not in good shape and only Rehoboam could make things better. Visitors to Israel were awestruck by what they saw, but they couldn't detect the moral and spiritual decay that was creeping through the foundations of the kingdom, beginning in the throne room.

The people were willing to serve Rehoboam if only he would serve them and make life a bit easier for them. All of God's truly great leaders had been servants to the people—Moses, Joshua, Samuel, and especially David—but Solomon had chosen to be a celebrity and not a servant, and Rehoboam was following his bad example. When the Son of God came to earth, He came as a servant (Luke 22:24-27; Phil. 2:1-13), and He taught His disciples to lead by serving. Jesus washed His disciples' feet as an example of humble service (John 13:1-17), and He wants us to follow His example, not the examples of the "great leaders" in the secular world (Matt. 20:25-28).

The advice of the counselors (vv. 6-11; 2 Chron. 10:6-11). Let's give Rehoboam credit for asking for a delay to give him time to think and seek counsel. However, time solves no problems; it's what leaders *do with time* that really counts. There's no evidence that the king sought the Lord in prayer or that he consulted with the high priest or with a prophet. We get the impression that his mind was already made up but that he was willing to go through the motions in order to please the people. One of the marks of David's leadership was that he was willing to humble himself and seek the mind of God, and then pray for God's blessing on his decisions. Leaders who try to impress people with their skills, but take no time to seek God, only prove that they don't know the most important thing in spiritual leadership: they are second in command. (See Josh. 5:13-15.)

In making important decisions, we should seek sound spiritual counsel (Prov. 11:14; 15:22; 24:6), but let's be sure the counselors we talk to are mature saints who are able to guide us aright. The British writer Frank W. Boreham said, "We make our decisions, and then our decisions turn around and make us." Sometimes we forget our decisions, but our decision can never forget us, because we reap what we sow. If the path we choose turns out to be a detour, then let's admit it, confess our sin, and ask the Lord to lead us back to the right road.

The elders gave Rehoboam the best advice: be a servant of the people and the people will serve you. However, Rehoboam had already made up his mind, so he immediately rejected that answer and turned to his contemporaries whom he knew would give him the answer that he wanted. He had no intention of weighing the facts, seeking God's will, and making the wisest choice. In more than fifty years of ministry, I've seen so-called Christian leaders take the Rehoboam approach, do terrible damage to the work of the Lord, and then walk away from the mess, leaving behind poison and debris that will take years to remove.

The ancient world honored age and maturity, but our modern society worships youth. In our churches and parachurch ministries, there's a desperate need for generational balance, with the older and younger generations communicating with each other and learning from each other, just like a family (Titus 2:1-8; 1 Tim. 5:1-2). A friend told me he wanted to start a church only for people fifty and older, and I suggested he put an undertaker on the staff. God meant for His church to include male and female, old and young, and those in between, and that all of them should learn from one another. There are old fools as well as young fools, and age is no guarantee of wisdom or even useful experience. The young people in my life help me catch up with the present, and I help them to catch up on the past, and so we all stay balanced and love one another.

The young counselors were interested primarily in being important and magnifying themselves and the authority of the new king. They thought the best way to do that was to make a show of force. Youth in general seeks to have authority and freedom, until they make the painful discovery that they may not be ready to use these precious gifts wisely. After admonishing both the elder saints and the younger ones, Peter wrote, "Yes, all of you be submissive to one another, and be clothed with humility, for 'God resists the proud, but gives grace to the humble'" (1 Peter 5:5, NKJV).

The announcement of the king (vv. 12-17; 2 Chron. 10:12-17). A man forty-one years old who had grown up in the palace, who had been given three days to consider a matter, and who even had access to those who could determine the will of God, should never have made this kind of a decision. His father had even written a book of practical proverbs about wisdom, one of which said, "A soft answer turns away wrath, but a harsh word stirs up anger" (Prov. 15:1, NKJV). However, Rehoboam's leadership was motivated by pride, not humility, and pride knows nothing of gentleness and kindness. "There is one who speaks like the piercings of a sword, but the tongue of the wise promotes health" (Prov. 12:18, NKJV). Apparently Rehoboam hadn't taken time to read and copy Deuteronomy 17:18-20.

The king answered the people roughly, which is the same Hebrew word that is translated "grievous" in verse 4. The way he spoke was rough and the words he used were harsh. Instead of lightening the yoke, Rehoboam announced that he would make it heavier and more cutting. His little finger was bigger than his father's waist, and if his father used whips, he would use scourges. ("Scorpions" was the name for a whip with metal pieces in it, similar to the Roman scourge.) Both in his words and his manner, the new king made it clear to the people that he was important and powerful and they were unimportant and weak, a dangerous message indeed.

Rehoboam represented the third generation of the Davidic dynasty, and so often it's the third generation that starts to tear down what the previous generations have built up. The people of Israel served the Lord during Joshua's days and during the days of the elders he had trained, but when the third generation came along, they turned to idols, and the nation fell apart (Jud. 2:7-10). I've seen this same phenomenon in businesses and local churches. The founders worked hard and sacrificed much to start the business or the church, and the second generation was faithful to the examples and beliefs of the founders. But when the third generation arrived, they inherited everything without working for it or paying for it, and they tore down what others had worked so hard to build up. Of course, if the second generation doesn't teach the third generation the ways of the Lord, or if they won't receive the teaching, it's no wonder the new generation goes astray (Deut. 11:18-21; 32:46; Eph. 6:4).

The consequences of Rehoboam's speech were predictable: "all Israel" (meaning the ten northern tribes)[4] announced their decision to leave the other two tribes and establish their own kingdom. They shouted the words of Sheba, a troublemaker in David's day (2 Sam. 20:1), left the assembly, and made Jeroboam their king. The only exceptions were the citizens of the ten tribes who had settled in Judah for one reason or another. They remained faithful to the throne of David.

Solomon's first official decision brought him the reputation for great wisdom (3:16-28), but his son's first official decision told the nation that he was foolish and unwise. For centuries, the Jews considered the division of the nation the greatest tragedy in their history and measured every other calamity by it (Isa. 7:17).

2. An angry king (1 Kings 12:18-24; 2 Chron. 10:18-19; 11:1-4)
While Rehoboam was still in Shechem, he attempted some belated diplomacy and sent one of his trusted officers to the assembled ten tribes to try to bring peace or at least keep the discussion going. His choice of mediators was unwise because Adoram was in charge of the forced labor, and forced labor was one of the irritating areas in the dispute.[5] Perhaps Adoram was authorized to negotiate easier labor arrangements or even lower

taxes, but if he was, he failed miserably. The people stoned him and the frightened king took off for Jerusalem as soon as he heard the news. Rehoboam had followed the wrong counsel, used the wrong approach, and chosen the wrong mediator. What else wrong could he do?

He could declare war!

After all, he was the king, and by declaring war he could assert his authority and demonstrate his military strength, and perhaps Jeroboam his rival might be one of the casualties. Didn't Solomon his father want to have Jeroboam killed (11:40), and wasn't his father the wisest man in the world? Didn't the ten northern tribes rebel against the king and even kill an innocent man whose only task was to encourage peace? The beloved King David declared war on the Ammonites for only *embarrassing* his envoys (2 Sam. 10), while Rehoboam's envoy was *murdered*. The ten northern tribes were dividing what the Lord had put together and they deserved to be chastised. They had even called an assembly and appointed Jeroboam as their king! To defy the covenants of God and desert the Davidic line was wicked. It seemed that every consideration pointed logically to one conclusion—war.

Every consideration except one: was this war the will of God? After Rehoboam had assembled an army of 180,000 men,[6] he discovered that he had wasted his time. The Lord sent the prophet Shemaiah[7] to tell the king to call off the fight and send the men home. Though what happened was the consequence of Rehoboam's foolishness and Jeroboam's aggressiveness, it was God who had ruled and overruled to bring about the division, thus fulfilling Ahijah's prophecy. Each man had acted freely and so had their counselors, yet the Lord's will was done. (See Acts 2:23.) Our sovereign God is so great that He had let people make their own decisions and yet accomplish His purposes.

The plan of God was only one factor; a second factor was that it was wrong for Judah and Benjamin to fight against their brothers (v. 24). It seems strange, yet family and national conflict appears repeatedly in the history of Israel. Abraham and Lot disagreed (Gen. 13), and Abraham reminded his nephew that they shouldn't fight because they were brothers (13:8). Jacob and Esau had a lifelong battle that their descendants continued for centuries (Gen. 27:41-46; Ps. 137:7; Obad. 10-13). Joseph's brothers hated him (Gen. 37), and Aaron and Miriam criticized their brother Moses (Num. 12). Saul was David's enemy and on many occasions tried to kill him. "Behold, how good and how pleasant it is for brethren to dwell together in unity" (Ps. 133:1, NKJV).[8]

Frequently in Old Testament history we find a prophet confronting a king with "Thus says the Lord." Whenever a king, a priest, or even another prophet stepped out of line, a prophet would step forward and rebuke him; and if the prophet's message was ignored, God's hand of judgment would fall. (See 1 Kings 13:21-22; 14:6-11; 16:1-4; 20:28ff; 2 Kings 1:16; 22:14-15.) Israel was to be a people of God's Word, and God's Word must be held higher than even the word of the king.

To Rehoboam's credit, he called off the attack, although in the years that followed, there were repeated border skirmishes and other irritating conflicts between Rehoboam and Jeroboam (14:20; and see 15:6, 16, 32; 2 Chron. 11:1). However, it's possible that Rehoboam was grateful that his plans never succeeded. Like his father, he wasn't a military man and he couldn't be sure of winning. It was God's plan there be two kingdoms, and that settled the matter. At least he submitted to the Word of God.

At this point in the record, the writer interrupted the Rehoboam story to tell us about Jeroboam. The Rehoboam account is amplified in 2 Chronicles 11:5-22 and then picked up and concluded in 1 Kings 14:21-36 (2 Chron. 12:1-16).

3. An astute king (2 Chron. 11:5-22)

Rehoboam heard and obeyed God's message from Shemaiah and the Lord began to give him wisdom and bless his life and his work. Had he stayed on that course, he would have led Judah into godliness and true greatness, but he turned from the Lord and lost the blessings he and his people could have enjoyed.[9]

God blessed his building projects (vv. 5-12). His father Solomon had strengthened the borders of the kingdom by putting up fortress cities for his soldiers, horses, and chariots (1 Kings 9:15-19; 2 Chron. 8:1-6), and Rehoboam followed his good example. The cities he selected formed a wall of protection for Jerusalem on the east and west and across the south. The king knew that Jeroboam was a favorite in Egypt, so perhaps he had Pharaoh in mind when he set up this line of defense. It's interesting that he didn't put defense cities across the northern border. After Shemaiah's warning, perhaps the king hesitated to provoke the northern tribes or to give the suggestion that Judah was preparing for war. He may have hoped that an "open door policy" would ease the tension and make it easier for the people in the ten tribes to come to Jerusalem.

God blessed his people (vv. 13-17). King Jeroboam ordained his own priests and turned the ten northern tribes into a center for worshiping idols, but for three years Rehoboam kept the people of Judah true to the Law of Moses. As a result, the priests and Levites in Israel who were devoted to the Lord came into Judah and enriched the nation greatly. Some priests and Levites merely "sided with Rehoboam" (v. 13) and remained in Israel, but others gave up their property in Israel and moved permanently to Judah (v. 14). A third group stayed in Israel but traveled to Jerusalem three times a year for the annual feasts (v. 16). (To some extent, we have these same three groups in the churches today.) The addition of these godly priests and Levites and their families to the population of Judah strengthened the kingdom and brought the blessing of the Lord. "Blessed is the nation whose God is the Lord; and the people whom he hath chosen as his own inheritance" (Ps. 33:12, KJV).

God blessed his family (vv. 18-23). Like both David and Solomon, Rehoboam disobeyed the Word and took many wives (Deut. 17:17). Only two of his wives are named in the record: Mahalath, a granddaughter of David through both her father and mother, and Maacah, the daughter of Absalom. Since David's son Absalom had only one daughter, Tamar (2 Sam. 14:27), Maacah could have been his granddaughter. Maacah's father's name is given as Abishalom in 1 Kings 15:2, and in 2 Chronicles 13:2, Maacha is called the daughter of Uriel of Gibeah. If this Uriel was indeed the husband of Tamar, the only daughter of Absalom, then Maacah was the granddaughter of Absalom and the great-granddaughter of King David. At least two of Rehoboam's eighteen wives were from solid Davidic stock.

It was important that kings and queens have large families so that there would be an heir to the throne and replacements if anything should happen to the crown prince. King Rehoboam was blessed with many children—twenty-eight sons and sixty daughters. The king did a very wise thing when he appointed his grown sons to royal offices and distributed them throughout Judah and Benjamin. This accomplished several things that made for peace and efficiency in the palace. To begin with, the princes weren't engaged in their own pursuits and getting involved in palace intrigues, as some of David's sons had done to the sorrow of their father. Rehoboam had grown up in the lap of luxury, but he was smart enough to put his sons to work.

The second benefit was that Rehoboam could assess their character and skills and decide which son would succeed him. God called David to be king and later told him that Solomon would be his successor. There's no evidence that God named Solomon's successor, so Solomon must have appointed Rehoboam to take the throne. After watching his sons, Rehoboam selected Abijah, son of Maacah,[10] to be his heir, even though Jeush, his son by Mahalath, with the firstborn (vv. 18-19). First, Rehoboam made Abijah "ruler among his brethren" (v. 22, KJV; "chief prince," NIV), which suggests that Abijah was his father's right-hand man, perhaps even coregent. Rehoboam recognized in this son the ability that was needed for a successful reign. Unfortunately, Abijah didn't live up to his name, "Jehovah is father."

The "many wives" that Rehoboam secured for his sons may have been "treaty wives" to guarantee peace between Judah and her neighbors. This was the plan his father Solomon followed.

4. An apostate king (1 Kings 14:21-31; 2 Chron. 12:1-16)

Rehoboam walked with the Lord for three years after becoming king (2 Chron. 11:17), but in the fourth year of his reign, when his throne was secure, he and all Judah turned away from Jehovah to worship idols (2 Chron. 12:1-2). "And he did evil, because he did not prepare his heart to seek the Lord" (2 Chron. 12:14, NKJV). The phrase "forsaken [abandoned] the commandment of the Lord" occurs frequently in the record of the reigns of the kings of Judah and Israel (1 Kings 18:18; 19:10, 14; 2 Kings 17:16; 21:22; 22:17; 2 Chron. 12:1, 5; 13:10-11; 15:2; 21:10; 24:18, 20, 24; 26:6; 29:6; 34:25). David had warned Solomon about this sin (1 Chron. 28:9, 20) and so had the Lord Himself (1 Kings 3:14; 9:4-9; 11:9-13), but Solomon in his latter years worshiped both the Lord and the abominable idols of the heathen. Solomon was influenced by his pagan wives to worship idols; perhaps Rehoboam was influenced by his Ammonite mother. Whatever the influence, the king knew that he was breaking the covenant and sinning against the Lord.

God's holy jealousy (vv. 21-24). When the Bible speaks of the Lord being "a jealous God" (14:22), it refers to His jealous love over His people, a love that will not tolerate rivals. Israel was "married" to the Lord at Mount Sinai when they entered into the covenant, and the worship of idols was a terrible breach of that covenant, like a wife committing adultery.[11] Surely Rehoboam knew what God said to the nation at Mount Sinai: "For I, the Lord your God, am a jealous God" (Ex. 20:5, NKJV). This same truth is included in The Song of Moses as well: "They have provoked Me to jealousy by what is not God; they have moved Me to anger by their foolish idols" (Deut. 32:21 NKJV; see also Ps. 78:58; Jer. 44:3). Paul used the marriage picture when he warned the church to avoid pagan idolatry (1 Cor. 10:22), and James called worldly believers "adulterers and adulteresses" (James 4:4, KJV).

The king allowed and encouraged the building of idolatrous shrines in the land ("high places"), the erecting of sacred stones ("images") and phallic images and Asherah poles ("groves"). He also permitted the shrine prostitutes, male ("sodomites") and female, to serve the people at these shrines, a detestable practice expressly forbidden by the Law of Moses (Deut. 23:17-18). Idolatry and immorality go together (Rom. 1:21-27), and it wasn't long before the pagan sins condemned by the law became commonly accepted practices in Judah (Lev. 18, 20; Deut. 18:9-12). The Jewish people were no longer a light to the Gentiles; instead, the darkness of the Gentiles had invaded the land and was putting out the light.

Before we pass judgment on the king and people of Judah, perhaps we had better examine our own lives and churches. Surveys indicate that, when it comes to sexual morality, the "born-again" people in the churches don't live much differently than the unsaved people outside the church. The materialistic and humanistic idols of the unsaved world have made their way into the church and are both tolerated and promoted. The Lord punished Rehoboam for his sins. How long will it be before the Lord punishes His church?

God's loving discipline (vv. 25-31; 2 Chron. 12:1-16). For a year, the Lord was patient with Rehoboam and the people of Judah; but by the fifth year of Rehoboam's reign, the long-suffering of the Lord had come to an end. God directed Shishak, king of Egypt, to invade Judah with a huge army and, in spite of Rehoboam's new defenses, he defeated town after town.[12] (One Egyptian inscription states that Shishak took 156 cities in Israel and Judah.) When the Egyptians got as far as Jerusalem, the prophet Shemaiah once again appeared on the scene with a message from God, short and to the point: "This is what the Lord says, 'You have abandoned me; therefore, I now abandon you to Shishak'" (12:5).

Whenever God's people experience discipline because of their sins, they can make a new beginning by hearing the Word of God and humbling themselves before the God of the Word. This was the promise God gave His people when Solomon dedicated the temple (2 Chron. 7:13-14). Rehoboam and his officers humbled themselves before the Lord and He stopped Shishak from attacking Jerusalem. However, Judah was now subject to Shishak and had to pay him tribute. God's people discovered that their "free-dom to sin" brought them into painful and costly bondage to Egypt, for the consequences of sin are always costly.

To satisfy Shishak's demands, Rehoboam gave him gold from the temple and from the king's palace. This included the five hundred gold shields that Solomon had made for the palace (1 Kings 10:16-17). Rehoboam was too poor to make duplicate shields, so he replaced them with shields made of bronze, and the royal ceremonies went on as if nothing had happened. How often the precious treasures of former generations are lost because of sin and then replaced by cheap substitutes. Life goes on and nobody seems to know the difference. That's what happened to the church at Laodicea (Rev. 3:17-19).

After the invasion of Shishak in 925 B.C., Rehoboam reigned for twelve more years and died in 913 B.C. Had he continued to walk with the Lord and to lead his people to be faithful to God's covenant, the Lord would have done great things for him. As it was, his sins and the sins of the people who followed him left the nation weaker, poorer, and in bondage. As Charles Spurgeon said, "God does not allow His people to sin successfully."

Rehoboam went the way of all flesh and died at the age of fifty-eight. We trust that the humbling that he and his leaders experienced lasted for the rest of their lives and that they walked with the Lord.

A New King, an Old Sin

King Jeroboam I[1] was a doer, not a philosopher; he was a man who first caught Solomon's attention because he was busy, efficient, dependable, and productive (11:26-28). He was the ideal popular leader who knew how to fight the people's battles and champion their causes. Ask him about his personal faith in the Lord and his answers might be a bit foggy. He had lived in Egypt long enough to develop a tolerance toward idolatry as well as an understanding of how religion can be used to control the people. In this skill, Jeroboam was one with Nebuchadnezzar (Dan. 3), Herod Agrippa I (Acts 12:19-25), and the Antichrist (Rev. 13, 17), and today's latest demagogue. But Jeroboam made three serious mistakes during his twenty-two-year reign.

1. He didn't believe God's promises (12:25-33)
Success in life depends on doing God's will and trusting God's promises, but Jeroboam failed in both. When Ahijah gave Jeroboam God's message that guaranteed him the throne of the kingdom of Israel (11:28-39), the prophet made it clear that political division did not permit religious departure. God would have given Jeroboam the entire kingdom except that He had

made an everlasting covenant with David to keep one of his descendants on the throne (2 Sam. 7:1-17). This protected the Messianic line so that the Savior could come into the world. The Lord tore the ten tribes away from Rehoboam because Rehoboam had followed Solomon's bad example and turned the people to idols. This should have been a warning to Jeroboam to be faithful to the Lord and stay away from false gods. The Lord also promised to build Jeroboam a "sure house" (a continued dynasty) if he obeyed the Lord and walked in His ways (v. 38, KJV). What a promise, yet Jeroboam couldn't believe it.

Fear (vv. 25-28). One of the first evidences of unbelief is fear. We get our eyes off the Lord and start looking at the circumstances. "Why are you fearful, O you of little faith?" Jesus asked His disciples (Matt. 8:23-27, NKJV), reminding them that faith and fear can't coexist in the same heart for very long. Jeroboam's fear was that the Southern Kingdom would attack him and his own people desert him and go back to Jerusalem to worship. The law not only appointed the temple in Jerusalem as the only place of sacrifice (Deut. 12), but it also commanded all Jewish men to go to Jerusalem three times a year to observe the appointed feasts (Ex. 23:14-17). What if the people decided to remain in Judah and not return to Israel? Even if they returned north after worshiping, how long could they live with divided loyalties? Perhaps Jeroboam recalled the plight of Saul's successor, Ish-Bosheth, who tried to rule over the ten northern tribes but failed and was slain (2 Sam. 4). If there was ever a popular movement in Israel toward uniting the two kingdoms, Jeroboam would be a dead man.

Security (v. 25). Like both Solomon (9:15-19; 11:27) and Rehoboam (2 Chron. 11:5-12), King Jeroboam fortified his capital city (Shechem) and strengthened other key cities against any invaders. Penuel (Peniel) was east of the Jordan and was famous as the place where Jacob wrestled with the angel of the Lord (Gen. 32). It appears that Jeroboam later moved his capital from Shechem to Tirzah (14:17), or perhaps he had a second palace there. Instead of trusting the Lord to be his shield and defender, Jeroboam trusted his own defenses and strategy.

Substitutes (vv. 26-33). The easiest solution to Jeroboam's problem of holding the loyalty of his people was to establish a worship center for them in the territory of Israel. But what authority did he have to devise a rival religion when the Jews had received their form of worship from the very hand of God? He certainly couldn't build a temple to compete with Solomon's temple in Jerusalem, or write a law that matched what Moses received from Jehovah, or set up a sacrificial system that would guarantee the forgiveness of sins. He was no Moses and he certainly couldn't claim to be God!

What Jeroboam did was to take advantage of the tendency of the Jewish people to turn to idols, and the desire of most people for a religion that is convenient, not too costly, and close enough to the authorized faith to be comfortable for the conscience. Jeroboam didn't tell the people to forget Jehovah but to worship Him in the form of a golden calf. In both Egypt and the land of Canaan, the king had seen statues of calves and bulls that were supposed to be "holding up" the invisible forms of the gods. In the pagan religions that Jeroboam was copying, calves and bulls symbolized fertility. Jeroboam turned his back on the most important message given at Mount Sinai: Israel's Lord Jehovah is a God who would be *heard* but not *seen* or *touched*. Hearing His Word is what generates faith (Rom. 10:17), and faith enables us to obey. But most people don't want to live by faith; they want to walk by sight and gratify their senses.

Jeroboam's words in verse 28 suggest that Aaron's golden calf (Ex. 32:1-8, especially v. 4) was also in his mind.[2] But the king went one better: he made *two* calves and put one at Bethel, on the farthest southern border of the kingdom, just a short distance from Jerusalem, and the other at Dan, on the farthest northern border (see Hos. 8:5-6; 13:2-3). Worshiping the Lord couldn't be more convenient! "It is too much for you to go up to Jerusalem," the king told the people (v. 28), and they were more than willing to believe him. The king built shrines at Bethel and Dan and allowed the people to make their own high places closer to home. By royal fiat, he instituted a "do-it-yourself religion" and, as in the Book of Judges, everybody did what was right in his own eyes (Jud. 17:6; 18:1; 19:1; 21:25). If the Canaanites and Egyptians could worship calves, so could the Hebrews! He forgot about Exodus 20:1-3 and 22–23—but the Lord's didn't forget!

A religion needs ministers, so Jeroboam appointed all kinds of people to serve as "priests" at the altars in Dan and Bethel (13:33-34; 2 Chron. 11:13-17). The only requirement was that each candidate bring with him a young bull and seven rams (2 Chron. 13:9).[3] God had made it clear when He gave Moses the law that only the sons of Aaron could serve as priests at the altar (Ex. 28:1-5; 29:1-9; 40:12-16) and that if anybody from another tribe tried to serve, he would be put to death (Num. 3:5-10). Even the Levites, who were from the tribe of Levi, were not allowed to serve at the altar on penalty of death (Num. 3:5-10, 38; 4:17-20; 18:1-7). Unauthorized priests at unauthorized temples could never have access to God or present sacrifices acceptable to God. It was a man-made religion that pleased the people, protected the king, and unified the nation—except for the faithful Levites who abandoned the Northern Kingdom and moved to Judah to worship God according to the teaching of the Scriptures (2 Chron. 11:13-17).

The law of Moses required the Jews to celebrate seven divinely appointed feasts each year (Lev. 23), so Jeroboam instituted a feast for the people of the Northern Kingdom. The Feast of Tabernacles was scheduled for the seventh month for one full week. This was a joyous festival when the people recalled their wilderness years by living in booths and celebrating the goodness of the Lord in giving the harvest. Jeroboam's feast was set for the eighth month so that the people had to choose which one they would attend, and this separated the loyal Jews from the counterfeit worshipers in Israel. But why travel all the way to Jerusalem when Bethel and Dan were much easier to reach?

Along with setting up his own religious calendar, temples, altars, and priesthood, Jeroboam made himself a priest (vv. 32-33)! He offered incense and blood sacrifices just as the authorized priests did at the temple, except that the Lord never acknowledged his sacrifices. The sacrifice on the fifteenth day of the eighth month was in connection with the feast that he had ordained, and this sacrifice may have been in imitation of the annual Day of Atonement. He had all the ingredients needed for a "religion" but lacked the most necessary one—the Lord God Jehovah!

Apostasy. We live today in an age when "manufactured religion" is popular, approved, and accepted. The blind leaders of the blind assert that we live in a "pluralistic society" and that nobody has the right to claim that only revelation is true and only one way of salvation is correct. Self-appointed "prophets" and ministers put together their own theology and pass it off as the truth. They aren't the least bit interested in what Scripture has to say; instead, they substitute their "feigned [plastic] words" (2 Peter 2:3, KJV) for God's unchanging and inspired Word, and many gullible people will fall for their lies and be condemned (2 Peter 2:1-2). Jeroboam's "religion" incorporated elements from the Law of Moses and from the pagan nations that the Jews had conquered. His system was what is today called "eclectic" (selective) or "syncretic" (combining many parts), but God called it heresy and apostasy. When the prophet Isaiah confronted the new religions in his day, he cried out, "To the law and to the testimony! If they do not speak according to this word, it is because there is no light in them" (Isa. 8:20, NKJV).

Because Jeroboam didn't believe God's promise given by the prophet Ahijah, he began to walk in unbelief and to lead the people into false religion. The religion he invented was comfortable, convenient, and not costly, but it wasn't authorized by the Lord. It was contrary to the revealed will of God in Scripture and it had as its purpose the unification of his kingdom, not the salvation of the people and the glory of God. It was man-made religion and God totally rejected it. Centuries later, Jesus told the woman of Samaria (the former kingdom of Israel), "You worship what you do not know; we worship that which we know, for salvation is from the Jews" (John 4:22, NASB). When He made that statement, He instantly wiped out every other religion and affirmed that the only way of salvation is from the Jews. Jesus was a Jew and the Christian faith was born out of the Jewish religion. Our modern "pluralistic society" notwithstanding, the Apostle Peter was right: "And there is salvation in no one else; for there is no other name under heaven that has been given among men, by which we must be saved"(Acts 4:12, NASB).

2. He didn't heed God's warnings (1 Kings 13:1-34)

This long chapter is not about young and old prophets; it's about King Jeroboam and his sins. The young prophet's ministry is very important in this account, for all that he said and experienced, including his death, were a part of God's warning to King Jeroboam. According to verse 33, the king didn't turn back to God: "After this event Jeroboam did not return from his evil ways" (NASB). In this chapter, a prophet died, but in the next chapter, the crown prince died! Obviously, God was trying to get Jeroboam's attention.

The message (vv. 1-2). The anonymous prophet came from Judah because there were still faithful servants of God there whom the Lord could use. He met Jeroboam at the shrine in Bethel, which eventually became "the king's sanctuary" (Amos 7:10-12). When you devise your own religion, as Jeroboam did, you can do whatever you please, and Jeroboam chose to be a priest as well as a king. Jeremiah and Ezekiel were priests who were called to be prophets, but the Mosaic Law didn't permit kings to serve as priests (2 Chron. 26:16-23). Jesus Christ is the only King who is also Priest (Heb. 7–8), and all who believe in Christ are "kings and priests" (Rev. 1:6, KJV) and "a royal priesthood" (1 Peter 2:9). Jeroboam's "priesthood" was spurious and rejected by the Lord. That may be why the anonymous prophet from Judah delivered his message while the king was at the altar.

The prophet spoke to the altar, not to the king, as though God no longer wanted to address Jeroboam, a man so filled with himself and his plans that he had no time to listen to God. The message declared that the future lay with the house of David, not with the house of Jeroboam. Because of Jeroboam's evil ways, the kingdom of Israel would become so polluted with idolatry and its accompanying sins that the kingdom would be wiped out within two centuries. In 722, the Assyrians captured Israel and the ten northern tribes moved off the scene.[4] David's dynasty continued until the reign of Zedekiah (597–586). He was Judah's last king before the Babylonian conquest of Jerusalem in 586.

The prophet's message looked ahead three hundred years to the reign of godly King Josiah (640–609) who rooted out the idolatry in the land, including the king's shrine at Bethel (2 Kings 23:15-16). Josiah desecrated the altar by burning human bones on it, and then he tore down the altar and let the ashes spill out. The prophecy was fulfilled just as the prophet announced. So sure was this promise that the prophet even named the king! (See also Isa. 44:28; 45:1, 13.)

The miracles (vv. 4-6). The king paid no attention to the message from God; all he wanted to do was punish the messenger. He was infuriated to hear that a king from Judah would one day desecrate and destroy his successful religious system. When Jeroboam stretched out his hand and pointed to the prophet, the Lord touched his arm and it suffered a stroke. What a humiliating experience for such a powerful king and priest! At that moment, the pagan altar split and the ashes came pouring out. Often the Lord authenticated His Word by giving miraculous signs (Heb. 2:1-4) but only to give emphasis to the message. In spite of Jeroboam's stubborn pride and willful disobedience, the Lord graciously healed his arm. (See Ex. 8:8; Acts 8:24.) It's too bad that the king was more concerned about physical healing for his body than moral and spiritual healing for his soul.

The king witnessed three miracles in just a few minutes, yet there's no evidence that he was convicted of his sins. Of themselves, miracles don't bring conviction or produce saving faith, but they do call attention to the Word. When Jesus raised Lazarus from the dead, some of the witnesses believed in Jesus while others went straight to the Jewish religious leaders and stirred up trouble (John 11:45-54). Miracles aren't necessary for evangelism (John 10:40-42), and those who claimed to believe on Christ only because of His miracles were really "unsaved believers" (John 2:23-25).

The maneuver (vv. 7-10). Jeroboam was a clever man and tried to trap the prophet by inviting him to the palace for a meal. Satan comes as the lion to devour us (1 Peter 5:8), and when that fails, he comes as a serpent to deceive us (2 Cor. 11:3; Gen. 3:1ff). The king's "Lay hold of him!" became "Come home with me!" But the prophet refused, for he knew his commission from the Lord compelled him to leave Bethel and not tarry. Had the prophet eaten a meal with the king, that one simple act would have wiped out the effectiveness of his witness and ministry. In the east, sharing a meal is a sign of friendship and endorsement. The prophet certainly didn't want to be a friend to such an evil man or give others the impression that he endorsed his wicked works. "Like a trampled spring and a polluted well is a righteous man who gives way before the wicked" (Prov. 25:26, NASB). A compromising servant of God muddies the waters and confuse the saints. The prophet refused the king's friendship, food, and gifts. Like Daniel, he said, "Let your gifts be for yourself, and give your rewards to another" (Dan. 5:17, NKJV).

The mistake (vv. 11-34). The faithful man from Judah couldn't be deceived by a wicked king but he could be fooled by an old retired prophet![5] This narrative presents some things to puzzle over, but we must not forget the main message: if the Lord punished a deceived prophet for his disobedience, how much more would he punish a wicked king who was sinning with his eyes wide open? If a true prophet disobeyed and was disciplined, what will happen to the false prophets? The prophet from Judah didn't compromise in his message, but he did compromise in his conduct, and he paid for his disobedience with his life. The Lord was saying to King Jeroboam, "If the righteous one is scarcely saved, where will the ungodly and the sinner appear?" (1 Peter 4:18, NKJV; see also Prov. 11:31).

There are some characteristics of the old prophet that bother me. First of all, what was he doing living in Bethel when by traveling just a few miles he could be in Judah? We get the impression that the prophet wasn't exactly a spiritual giant, otherwise the Lord would have called him to rebuke the king. The fact that he lied to a fellow prophet raises some questions about his character. It's also disturbing that he wept over the younger man's death *when he helped to cause it*, and then buried the man he helped to kill. Was he trying to atone for his own sins against the prophet?

The younger prophet did his work well and got out of town. Had he kept going and not lingered under the tree he would have escaped the tempting offer of the old prophet. God's servants often face great temptations after times of great success and excitement. (See 1 Kings 18 and 19.) The old man's sons witnessed the confrontation with Jeroboam at the altar and told their father what the prophet from Judah had said about the king and about his commission from the Lord (vv. 8-10). When the old prophet caught up with the messenger of the Lord, he deliberately tempted him to disobey the Lord's commission, *and the younger man fell into the trap!* The older prophet should not have tempted a fellow servant to disobey, but the younger man shouldn't have hastened to accept the older man's words. If God gave the man from Judah the message and the instructions for delivering it, then God could also give him the changes in the plan.

When an emotionally disturbed man told Charles Spurgeon that God had told him to preach for Spurgeon the next Sunday at the Metropolitan Tabernacle, Spurgeon replied, "When the Lord tells me, I'll let you know." Other believers can use the Word to encourage us, warn us, and correct us, but *beware of letting other believers tell you God's will for your life*. The Father loves each of His children personally and wants to convey His will to each personally (Ps. 33:11). Yes, there's safety in a multitude of counselors, provided they're walking with the Lord, but there's no certainty that you have the will of God just because a committee approved it.

Since he knew what the prophet from Judah was supposed to do, why did the old man deliberately lie to the young man and encourage him to disobey the Lord? Was the old man worried that the visiting prophet might stir things up in comfortable Bethel and create problems for him and other satisfied compromisers? Perhaps the young prophet was feeling proud of what he had done—preaching a powerful message and performing three miracles—and the Lord used the old man to test him and bring him back to essentials. By telling the lie, the old prophet tempted the young man, but by going back to Bethel, the young prophet tempted himself (he was out of God's will) and tempted the Lord. Why didn't the young visitor seek the face of the Lord and find out His will? The text tells us only the events, not the motives in the hearts of the participants, so we can't answer any of these questions with finality.

One of the strangest events of all is that the Lord sent His Word to the old prophet who was out of His will! But God spoke to Balaam, who was not necessarily a separated and dedicated man, as well as to Elijah (1 Kings 18) and Jonah (Jonah 3–4). After the meal, the younger prophet started back home and the lion met him and killed him. But even this event had miracle aspects to it, because the lion didn't maul the body or attack the mule, and the mule didn't run away. The animals must have remained there a long time because witnesses told the tale in Bethel and people came out to see the sight, including the old prophet who carried the body away and buried it. Surely the news arrived at the palace, and perhaps the king rejoiced that his enemy was dead. But the prophet's words were not dead! And the very death of the prophet was another warning to Jeroboam that he had better start to obey the Word of God.

The old prophet must have recovered his courage, for he publicly declared that the prophecy given at the Bethel altar would be fulfilled (vv. 31-32), and it was (2 Kings 23:15-18). Three hundred years later, King Josiah saw the old prophet's tomb and took courage that the Lord does fulfill His Word. But did any of these unusual events convict the heart of King Jeroboam and bring him to a place of repentance? "But even after this, Jeroboam did not turn from his evil ways" (v. 33, NLT). However, God's next warning would come closer to home.

3. He didn't receive God's help (1 Kings 14:1-20)

We don't read in Scripture that Jeroboam sought the Lord's will, prayed for spiritual discernment, or asked the Lord to make him a godly man. He prayed for healing for his arm, and now he asked the prophet Ahijah to heal his son, the crown prince and heir to the throne. It's obvious that physical blessings were more important to him than spiritual blessings. Like many nominal believers and careless church members today, the only time Jeroboam wanted help from God's servant was when he was in trouble.

The pretending wife (vv. 1-3). Abijah wasn't a little child at this time. He was old enough to be approved by the Lord (v. 13) and appreciated by the people, for they mourned over him when he died (v. 18). No doubt the godly remnant in Israel pinned their hopes on the young prince, but God judged the royal family and the apostate citizens by calling the boy away from the cesspool of iniquity that was called Israel. "The righteous man perishes, and no man takes it to heart; and devout men are taken away, while no one understands. For the righteous man is taken away from evil" (Isa. 57:1, NASB).

The king wanted help from the prophet, but he was too proud to admit it or to face Ahijah personally. The prophet still lived in Shiloh (11:29) because he was too old and infirm to relocate in Judah, and he wanted to be faithful to the very end and warn Jeroboam of the consequences of his sins. Did the king think a disguise would fool the godly prophet, blind as he was? Ahijah could see more in his blindness than Jeroboam and his wife could see with their gift of sight.[6] The gifts the queen carried were those of a common laborer, not gifts fit for a king to give.

The discerning prophet (vv. 4-6). It was about twenty miles from Tirzah to Shiloh, but the prophet knew she was coming before she even arrived in the city. The aged prophet knew who was coming, why she was coming and what he was supposed to tell her. "The secret of the Lord is with those who fear Him" (Ps. 25:14, NKJV). "Surely the Lord does nothing, unless He reveals His secret to His servants the prophets" (Amos 3:7, NKJV). Jeroboam sent his wife to Ahijah, but Ahijah said that he was

111

sent to her! He gave her the message she was to give to her husband, and it wasn't a very happy one.

The revealing message (vv. 7-16). First, the prophet reminded Jeroboam of *God's grace in the past (vv. 7-8a).* The Lord had chosen Jeroboam and raised him from being a district leader to ruling over the Northern Kingdom.[7] God had torn ten tribes away from the house of David and had given them to Jeroboam. But then Ahijah revealed *Jeroboam's sins in the present (vv. 8b-9).* Unlike David, who had a heart wholly dedicated to the Lord, Jeroboam did more evil than Saul, David, and Solomon put together. He turned from the true God of Israel and made false gods, and then allowed the people of the ten tribes to worship them. He organized a counterfeit religion, provoked the Lord to anger, and refused to listen to the prophets who were sent to warn him.

This led to Ahijah's *revelation of Jeroboam's future (vv. 10-16).* To begin with, unlike King David, Jeroboam would not establish a dynasty, even though God had promised to bless him with a "sure house" if he obeyed the Lord (11:38, KJV). All of Jeroboam's male descendants would be cut off; the Lord would make a "clean sweep" of Jeroboam's family and take away every potential heir, just the way servants remove dung from a house. (God didn't think much of the king's children!) But even worse, none of them except Abijah, the ailing crown prince, would have a decent dignified burial. Between the scavenger dogs in the city and the carrion birds in the fields, the children's corpses would be devoured and never buried, a terrible humiliation for any Jew.

Then Ahijah got to the matter at hand, the future of the sick heir to the throne. Abijah would die, have a dignified burial, and be mourned by the people. The one son of wicked Jeroboam who could have ruled justly would be taken from them, not because he was wicked but because he was good and God wanted to spare him the suffering that lay ahead of the kingdom (Isa. 57:1). As he looked ahead (v. 14), Ahijah then saw Nadab, Jeroboam's son and heir, reign for two years and then be assassinated by Baasha, a man from the tribe of Issachar (15:25-31). Baasha would not only kill Nadab, but he would exterminate the family of

Jeroboam, in fulfillment of Ahijah's prophecy (15:29).

But then the blind prophet looked even further ahead (vv. 15-16) and saw the entire kingdom of Israel defeated by the enemy (Assyria), rooted out of the land, and scattered among the nations. This happened in 722 B.C. The kingdom of Israel had a new religious system, but they were still under the Lord's covenant (Lev. 26; Deut. 28–30). That covenant warned that their disobedience to God's law would bring military defeat and national dispersion to the nation (Deut. 28:25-26, 49-52; Lev. 26:17, 25, 33-39; and see Deut. 7:5 and 12:3-4). What would be the cause of this terrible judgment? "[T]he sins of Jeroboam, who did sin, and who made Israel to sin" (v. 16, KJV). Just as David was God's standard for measuring the good kings, Jeroboam was God's example of the worst of the bad kings. See 1 Kings 15:34; 16:2-3, 7, 19, 26, 31; 22:52; 2 Kings 3:3; 9:9; 10:29, 31; 13:2, 6, 11; 14:24; 15:9, 18, 24, 28; 17:21-22.

The distressing fulfillment (vv. 17-20). Jeroboam apparently had a palace in Tirzah as well as the palace in Shechem, and it must have been at the edge of the city. Ahijah had told Jeroboam's wife that the child would die as soon as she entered the city (v. 12), but v. 17 indicates that he died when she stepped on the threshold of the door. All Israel did mourn the loss of this son and they gave him a funeral suited to a crown prince. The king's hand had been healed and his altar destroyed (13:1-16), and now his son had died. His army would be defeated by the king of Judah, also named Abijah (2 Chron. 13). How many times did God have to warn him before he would repent?

Nobody could sin like Jeroboam, son of Nebat. During his twenty-two years as king of Israel, he led his family and the nation into ruin. One day Jeroboam died and was succeeded by his son Nadab who was assassinated. The day would come when not a single male descendant of King Jeroboam would be alive, nor would you be able to identify the ten tribes of Israel.

"Indeed I tremble for my country when I reflect that God is just; that His justice cannot sleep forever. . . ."[8] Thomas Jefferson wrote those words in 1781, but they are just as applicable to us today.

NINE

1 KINGS 15:1–16:28
[2 CHRONICLES 13–16]

Kings on Parade

Were it not for the overruling hand of a sovereign God, the Jewish nation could never have accomplished what God called them to do: bearing witness of the one true and living God, writing the Scriptures, and bringing the Savior into the world. There were now two kingdoms instead of one, and leaders and common people in both kingdoms had departed from the Lord to serve idols. The priests still carried on the temple ministry in Judah, but during the 345 years from Rehoboam to Zedekiah, only eight of Judah's nineteen kings were classified as "good." As for Israel's twenty kings, for the most part they were all self-seeking men who were classified as "evil." Some were better than others, but none was compared with David.

Keep in mind that the books of Kings and Chronicles don't record history from exactly the same perspective. The focus in 1 and 2 Kings is on the kings of Israel, but in 1 and 2 Chronicles, the emphasis is on David's dynasty in Judah. The Northern Kingdom of Israel, later called Samaria, is mentioned in Chronicles only when it had dealings with Judah. Another thing to remember is that the two kingdoms used different systems in keeping official records. In Judah, the king's reign was counted from the beginning of the next calendar year after he began his reign, while in Israel, the count began with the year the king actually ascended the throne. Also, some kings had their sons as co-regents during the closing years of their reign. These factors complicate calculating how long some kings reigned, and this helps us understand why biblical chronologists don't always agree.

1. A dynasty continues (1 Kings 15:1-24; 2 Chron. 13–16)
The Northern Kingdom of Israel had nine dynasties in about 250 years while the Southern Kingdom faithfully maintained the Davidic dynasty for 350 years, and that was the dynasty from which the Lord Jesus Christ, the Son of David, would come (Matt. 1:1). With all of its faults, the kingdom of Judah was identified with the true and living God, practiced authorized worship in the temple, and had kings who came from David's family. Two of these kings are named in these chapters—Abijah and Asa.

Abijah (vv. 1-8; 2 Chron. 13). This son of Rehoboam was handpicked by his father because of his proven ability (2 Chron. 11:22), but he wasn't a godly man (15:3). He reigned only three years (913–910). He was from David's line through both parents, for David's infamous son Absalon was Abijah's paternal grandfather. Abijah may have had David's blood flowing in his veins, but he didn't have David's perfect heart beating in his breast. Abijah's father Rehoboam had kept up a running war with Jeroboam, and Abijah carried on the tradition.

However, Abijah knew his history and had faith in what God said to Moses and David. He had the courage to preach a sermon to Jeroboam and his army of 800,000 men, twice as large as Judah's army, reminding them of the true foundation for the Jewish faith (2 Chron. 13:4ff). For his platform, he used Mount Zemaraim, a prominent place located on the border between Benjamin and Israel (Josh. 18:22). He opened his sermon by reminding Jeroboam that the line of David was the true royal dynasty as stated in God's unchanging covenant with David (vv. 4-5; 2 Sam. 7) The phrase "covenant of salt" means "a perpetual covenant" (Num. 18:19).

Anticipating the argument that the Lord had also made Jeroboam king, Abijah explained why the nation divided (2 Chron. 13:6-7). Jeroboam had rebelled against both Solomon and Rehoboam and had to flee to Egypt to be safe. Then Rehoboam, in his immaturity, listened to unwise counsel and made a foolish decision that led to Jeroboam becoming king.[1] But God's original plan was that the line of David would reign over a united kingdom. In 1 and 2 Chronicles, the emphasis is on the legitimacy of the Davidic dynasty (1 Chron. 17:14; 28:5; 29:11, 23; 2 Chron. 9:8).

Having settled the matter that the sons of David should sit on the throne, Abijah reminded Jeroboam that only the sons of Aaron could serve in the temple (2 Chron. 13:8-12). The only divinely authorized temple of the Lord was in Jerusalem, and there the priests, the sons of Aaron, conducted the form of worship commanded by the Lord through Moses. Judah worshiped the one true and living God, while Israel worshiped two golden calves. Israel's priests were hirelings, not divinely appointed servants of the Lord. In Judah, the people honored the Lord God Jehovah. "God himself is with us!" Therefore, if Israel attacked Judah, Israel was fighting against the Lord!

Abijah's sentries weren't doing a very good job, for while Abijah was speaking, some of Jeroboam's soldiers moved behind him and set up an ambush. If Judah did attack, they'd find their smaller army fighting on two fronts, surely a dangerous situation. It's important to have good theology, but it's also important to have good strategy and alert guards on duty. But Abijah was up to the challenge and he cried out to God for deliverance. At the same time, the priests blew their trumpets (Num. 10:8-10) and the army of Judah gave a great shout, just as the people had done at Jericho (Josh. 6), and the Lord sent immediate victory.[2] Over half of Jeroboam's army was slain by the army of Judah, and Abijah's soldiers moved north to capture the city of Bethel, ten miles from Jerusalem. From Bethel they moved five miles north and took Jeshanah and four miles northeast to take Ephrain (Ephron). Abijah not only defeated the army of Israel and recovered some lost territory, but he gave Jeroboam a blow from which he never recovered. Then the Lord struck Jeroboam and he died (2 Chron. 13:20; 1 Kings 14:19-20).

It was for the glory of His own name that the Lord acted as He did. In 1 Kings, Abijah isn't marked out as a godly ruler, but we commend him for his understanding of God's truth and his faith in God's power. Abijah was no Joshua, but the God of Joshua was still the God of His people and proved Himself faithful. Abijah become more and more powerful, fathered many children, and helped to continue the dynasty of David. God uses imperfect people to do His will, if only they will trust Him.

Asa (vv. 9-24; 2 Chron. 14–16). Abijah's son Asa ruled for forty-one years (910–869). He began his reign with a heart like that of David (1 Kings 15:11; 2 Chron. 14:2), but though a good king for most of his life, during the last five years of his reign, he rebelled against the Lord. The word "mother" in 15:10 (KJV) should be "grandmother" for it refers to the same person mentioned in v. 2. The Jewish people didn't identify relatives with the same precision we do today. There were three major divisions to Asa's life and reign.

(1) Peace and victory (1 Kings 15:9-11; 2 Chron. 14:1–15:7). Thanks to his father's victory over Jeroboam (2 Chron. 13), Asa had peace during the first ten years of his reign (2 Chron. 14:1). During that time, he led a national reformation, cleansed the land of idolatry, and urged the people to seek the Lord (vv. 2-5). He also fortified the land by building defense cities and assembling an army of 580,000 men (vv. 6-8). The emphasis, however, wasn't on military achievements but on seeking the Lord (v. 7). It was God who gave them peace because they sought His face. They used that time of peace to prepare for any war that might occur, for faith without works is dead. It's a good thing Asa was prepared, because the Egyptian army attacked Judah, led by Zerah, who was a Cushite. The two armies met at Mareshah, about twenty-five miles southwest of Jerusalem.

Like his father, Asa knew how to call on the Lord in the day of trouble (14:11; 13:14-18). The king wasn't ignorant of his plight, because he identified Judah as "those who have no power." Zerah's army was almost twice as large as Asa's, and Asa's men had no chariots. Whether by many soldiers or by few, the Lord could work in mighty power. He may have had the words of Jonathan in mind when he prayed that way (1 Sam. 14:6). He might also have been thinking of what Solomon asked in his prayer of dedication (2 Chron. 6:34-35). Sudden deliverance in the midst of battle is a repeated theme in 2 Chronicles (13:14-18; 14:11-12; 18:31; 20:1ff; 32:20-22).

Asa's motive wasn't simply to defeat a dangerous enemy but to bring glory to Jehovah. Like David approaching Goliath, he attacked the enemy army "in the name of the Lord of hosts, the God of the armies of Israel" (1 Sam. 17:45, KJV). In response to Asa's prayer of faith, the Lord soundly defeated the Egyptian army and enabled Asa and his men to pursue them south to Gerar. There the men of Judah and Benjamin plundered the cities around Gerar and brought back an immense amount of spoils. This defeat of the Egyptian army was so thorough and so humiliating that the Egyptians didn't attack the people of Judah again until nearly three hundred years later when King Josiah met the forces of Pharaoh Neco at Carchemish (2 Chron. 35:20-24).

The Lord sent the prophet Azariah to meet Asa and the victorious army and give them a message of encouragement and warning (see also 1 Kings 12:21-24; 2 Chron. 16:7). More than one general has won a battle but afterwards lost the war because of pride or carelessness, and the Lord didn't want Asa to fall into that trap. Azariah's message was the same as that of King Asa: seek the Lord, obey Him, trust Him, and be strong in the Lord (2 Chron. 15:1-7; see also 14:4 and Deut. 4:29). Azariah reviewed the the dark days of the judges, when the nation didn't have a king, a godly priest, or anyone to enforce the law (Jud. 2:11-21). Because the people had turned to idols, their land was overrun by the enemy and it wasn't safe to travel (Jud. 5:6; 19:20). This was a fulfillment of God's covenant warning (Deut. 28:25-26, 30, 49-52). But whenever the people cried out to God and forsook their idols, He mercifully forgave them and defeated the enemy.

Azariah admonished the king and the people to get to work, build the nation, and serve the Lord faithfully.

(2) Reformation and renewal (1 Kings 15:12-15; 2 Chron. 15:8-19). This is the second phase of Asa's reformation, and certainly he dealt more severely with sin in the land than in the first phase. He expelled the shrine male prostitutes, for this practice was prohibited by God's law (Deut. 23:17), as was sodomy itself (Lev. 18:22; 20:13; see also Rom. 1:27 and 1 Cor. 6:9). He also removed his own grandmother from being the queen mother because she had an idolatrous shrine in a grove. That took some courage! We aren't told where this dedicated wealth had been kept, but Asa brought it to the temple treasury because it had been dedicated to the Lord. This was probably booty taken from the enemies he and his father had defeated with the Lord's help.

Once again, he removed the idols from the land, and he also repaired the altar of sacrifice that stood in the court of the priests before the temple. How or why the altar was damaged, the text doesn't say; but without the altar, the priests had no place to offer sacrifices. Solomon dedicated the temple in about 959, and Asa's fifteenth year was 896 (2 Chron. 15:10), so the altar had been in constant use for over sixty years. Perhaps it was just worn out, but a neglected altar isn't a very good testimony to the state of religion in the land. The Hebrew word can also mean "to renew," so perhaps the altar was rededicated to the Lord.

It's one thing to remove idols and repair the altar, but the greatest need was to rededicated the people. In the fifteenth year of his reign, Asa called for a great assembly to gather at Jerusalem to worship the Lord and renew the covenant.[3] Not only did the people of Judah and Benjamin attend, but devout people came to Jerusalem from Ephraim, Manasseh, and Simeon. The thing that drew them was the obvious fact that the Lord was with Asa. Since they assembled in the third month, they were probably celebrating the Feast of Pentecost (Lev. 23:15-22). The king brought the spoils of battle to be dedicated to the Lord, including valuable metals (1 Kings 15:15) and animals for sacrifice (2 Chron. 15:11).

At significant times throughout Jewish history you find the leaders and the people renewing their commitment to the Lord, a good example for the church to follow today. After the nation crossed the Jordan and entered the land, they renewed their covenant with the Lord (Josh. 8:30ff). Joshua called for a similar meeting near the close of his life (Josh. 24). When Saul was named king, Samuel called for an assembly and a time of renewal (1 Sam. 11:14–12:25). King Joash and King Josiah both renewed the covenant between themselves and the people and God (2 Kings 11:4ff; 23:1ff). Spiritual revival or renewal doesn't mean asking God for something new but for the renewal of our devotion to that which He has already given to us. Asa didn't reorganize the priesthood or remodel the temple, nor did he import new worship ideas from the pagan nations around him. He simply led the people in rededication to the covenant that God had already given them. They sought the Lord with all their hearts and He heard them.[4] God was pleased with this new step of commitment and He gave Judah and Benjamin peace for another twenty years.

(3) Relapse and discipline (1 Kings 15:16-24; 2 Chron. 16:1-14). Apparently King Asa had become careless in his walk with the Lord, because the Lord sent Baasha, king of Israel, to war against him.[5] Baasha fortified Ramah, which was located about six miles north of Jerusalem. From this outpost he would be able to monitor his own people who might go to Jerusalem and also launch his own attack on Judah.

After all that the Lord had done for Asa, you would think he would have called the people together to confess sin, seek the Lord, and learn His will about this serious situation. But instead, in his unbelief, he resorted to politics. He took the dedicated treasures from the temple and gave them to Ben-hadad, king of Syria, and entered into a pact with a pagan nation. (David had defeated Syria! See 2 Sam. 8:3-12 and 1 Chron. 18:3-4.) With Syria attacking Israel from the north, Baasha would have to abandon Ramah and move north to defend his country. King Asa not only followed the bad example of his father Abijah in making an unholy alliance, but he insisted that Ben-hadad lie and break his treaty with Israel! Scripture doesn't tell us when Abijah made a pact with Ben-hadad, but perhaps he married one of the Syrian princesses and in that way secured peace, following the example of Solomon (2 Chron. 13:21).

Ben-hadad took the silver and gold, broke his promise with Israel, and helped Judah. He captured the cities of Ijon, Dan, and Abelmaim in the north, and then marched through the tribe of Naphtali and took all the important storage cities. In this way, he gained control over the major trade routes and crippled Baasha's power and income. Having achieved his purpose, Asa conscripted the people to go to Ramah and carry off the stones and timber, and with that material the king built two fortified cities: Mizpeh about two and a half miles north of Ramah, and Geba about the same distance to the east. Judah had extended its border as far as Bethel (2 Chron. 13:17), and these new military sites would make their position even more secure.

Everyone was happy with the results of the treaty except the Lord. He sent the prophet Hanani to rebuke the king and give him the Word of the Lord. It was the task of the prophet to rebuke kings and other leaders, including priests, when they had disobeyed the law of the Lord. The prophet's message was clear: if Asa had relied on the Lord, the army of Judah would have defeated both Israel and Syria. Instead, Judah merely gained a few towns, the Lord's treasury was robbed and the king was now in a sinful alliance with the Syrians. Hanani reminded Asa that the Lord hadn't failed him when Zerah and the huge Egyptian army attacked Judah. The king had done a foolish thing in hiring the Syrians. Judah would pay for his mistake for years to come, and Syria did become a constant problem to the kingdom of Judah.

The fundamental problem was not Judah's lack of defenses but the king's lack of faith. Unlike David, whose heart was sincere before the Lord (see 1 Kings 15:5, 11), Asa's heart was divided—one day trusting the Lord and the next day trusting in the arm of flesh. A perfect heart isn't a sinless heart but a heart wholly yielded to the Lord and fully trusting Him. King Asa revealed the wickedness of his heart by becoming angry, rejecting the prophet's message, and putting him in prison. Apparently some of the people opposed Asa's foreign policy and his mistreatment of God's servant, so the king brutally oppressed them.

God gave Asa time to repent, but he refused to do so. In the thirty-ninth year of Asa's reign, the Lord afflicted him with a disease in his feet, which must have brought him considerable pain and inconvenience. Once again, he turned his back on the Lord and refused to confess his sins and seek Jehovah, but he turned for help to his physicians. Two years later, he died, and the throne was given to his son Jehoshaphat, who had probably served as coregent during the last years of his father's life.[6] Asa was a man who made a good beginning and lived a life of faith, but when it came to his final years, rebelled against the Lord. The people made a very great bonfire in his honor, but in God's sight, the last years of Asa went up in smoke (1 Cor. 3:13-15).[7]

2. A dynasty concludes (1 Kings 15:25–16:22)

At this point, the historian turns to the account of the kings of Israel and will remain there until the end of the book. The story of the kings of Judah is found primarily in 2 Chronicles. David's dynasty is mentioned in 1 and 2 Kings only where there is some interaction between Judah and Israel. The dynasty that began with Jeroboam is now about to end.

Nadab is assassinated (15:25-31). Jeroboam reigned over Israel for 22 years (14:20) and became the prime example in Scripture of an evil king (see 15:34; 16:2, 19, 26, etc.). Nadab inherited his father's throne as well as his father's sinful ways. He had reigned only two years when a conspiracy developed that led to King Nadab being assassinated by Baasha, a man from Issachar. Nadab was with the army of Israel, directing the siege of Gibbethon, a Philistine city south of Ekron. This border city had been a source of friction between Israel and the Philistines. It actually belonged to the tribe of Dan (Josh. 19:43-45) and was a Levitical city (Josh. 21:23), and Nadab wanted to reclaim it for Israel.

Baasha not only killed the king but he seized his throne and proceeded to fulfill the prophecy of Ahijah that Jeroboam's family would be completely wiped out because of the sins Jeroboam committed (14:10-16). Had Jeroboam obeyed God's Word, he would have enjoyed the blessing and help of the Lord (11:38-39), but because he sinned and caused the nation to sin, the Lord had to judge him and his descendants. That was the end of the dynasty of Jeroboam I.

Baasha disobeys God (15:32–16:7). Baasha set up his palace at Tirzah and reigned over Israel for twenty-four years. Instead of avoiding the sins that brought about the extinction of Jeroboam's family—and he was the man who killed them—Baasha copied the lifestyle of his predecessor! It has well been said that the one thing we learn from history is that we don't learn from history. Baasha had destroyed Jeroboam's dynasty, but he couldn't destroy the Word of God. The Lord sent the prophet Jehu to give the king the solemn message that after he died, his family would be exterminated, and another dynasty would be destroyed because of the father's sin. Baasha's descendants would be slain and their corpses become food for the dogs and the vultures. For a Jew's body not to be buried was a terrible form of humiliation.[8]

Elah is assassinated (16:8-14). Baasha had a normal death, but his son and successor did not. Elah appears to be a dissolute man who would rather get drunk with his friends than serve the Lord and the people. Arza was probably the prime minister. Both men forgot the words of Solomon, who knew a thing or two about kingship: "Woe to you, O land, when your king is a child, and your princes feast in the morning! Blessed are you, O land, when your king is the son of nobles, and your princes feast at the proper time—for strength and not for drunkenness" (Ecc. 10:16-17, NKJV).

The assassin this time is Zimri, the captain of half of the charioteers in the army of Israel. As a noted captain, he had access to the king, and what better time to kill him than when he was drunk? Like Elah's father, Zimri seized the throne, and once he was in power, he killed every member of Baasha's family. Baasha had fulfilled the prophecy of Abijah and Zimri fulfilled the prophecy of Jehu. But it must be pointed out that a person who fulfills divine prophecy is not innocent of sin. Both Baasha and Zimri were murderers and guilty of regicide, and the Lord held them responsible and accountable. The dynasty of Jeroboam was no more and the dynasty of Baasha was no more. In Judah, the dynasty of David continued.

T E N

Let the Fire Fall!

Elijah the Tishbite[1] suddenly appears on the scene and then leaves as quickly as he came, only to reappear three years later to challenge the priests of Baal. His name means "The Lord (Jehovah) is my God," an apt name for a man who called the people back to the worship of Jehovah (18:21, 39). Wicked King Ahab had permitted his wife Jezebel to bring the worship of Baal into Israel (16:31-33) and she was determined to wipe out the worship of Jehovah (18:4). Baal was the Phoenician fertility god who sent rain and bountiful crops, and the rites connected with his worship were unspeakably immoral. Like Solomon who catered to the idolatrous practices of his heathen wives (11:1-8), Ahab yielded to Jezebel's desires and even built her a private temple where she could worship Baal (16:32-33). Her plan was to exterminate the worshipers of Jehovah and have all the people of Israel serving Baal.

The prophet Elijah is an important figure in the New Testament. John the Baptist came in the spirit and power of Elijah (Luke 1:17), and some of the people even thought he was the promised Elijah (John 1:21; Mal. 4:5-6; Matt. 17:10-13). Elijah was with Moses and Jesus on the Mount of Transfiguration

(Matt. 17:3), and some students believe that Moses and Elijah are the two witnesses described in Rev. 11:1-14. Elijah wasn't a polished preacher like Isaiah and Jeremiah, but was more of a rough-hewn reformer who challenged the people to abandon their idols and return to the Lord. He was a courageous man who confronted Ahab personally and rebuked his sin, and he also challenged the priests of Baal to a public contest. He was not only a worker of miracles, but he also experienced miracles in his own life. These two chapters record seven different miracles that Elijah either performed or experienced.

1. A nationwide drought (1 Kings 17:1)

The Jewish people depended on the seasonal rains for the success of their crops. If the Lord didn't send the early rain in October and November and the latter rain in March and April, there would soon be a famine in the land. But the blessing of the semi-annual rains depended on the people obeying the covenant of the Lord (Deut. 11). God warned the people that their disobedience would turn the heavens into bronze and the earth into iron (Deut. 28:23-24; see Lev. 26:3-4, 18-19). The land belonged to the Lord, and if the people defiled the land with their sinful idols, the Lord wouldn't bless them.

It's likely that Elijah appeared before King Ahab in October, about the time the early rains should have begun. There had been no rain for six months, from April to October, and the prophet announced that there would be no rain for the next three years![2] The people were following Baal, not Jehovah, and the Lord could not send the promised rain and still be faithful to His covenant. God always keeps His covenant, whether to bless the people for their obedience or to discipline them for their sins.

God had held back the rain because of the fervent prayers of Elijah, and He would send the rain again in response to His servant's intercession (James 5:17-18). For the next three years, the word of Elijah would control the weather in Israel! The three and a half years of drought would prepare the people for the dramatic contest on Mount Carmel between the priests of Baal and the prophet of the Lord. Like a faithful servant, attentive to his master's commands, Elijah stood before the Lord and served him. (Later, his successor Elisha would use this same terminology. See 2 Kings 3:14 and 5:16.) An extended drought, announced and controlled by a prophet of Jehovah, would make it clear to everybody that Baal the storm god was not a true god at all.

2. Food from unclean birds (1 Kings 17:2-7)

After Elijah left the king's presence, Jezebel must have instigated her campaign to wipe out the prophets of the Lord (18:4). As the drought continued and famine hit the land, Ahab began his search for Elijah, the man he thought caused all the trouble (18:17). In one sense, Elijah did cause the drought, but it was the sins of Ahab and Jezebel that led the nation into disobeying God's covenant and inviting His chastening. The Lord had a special hiding place for His servant by a brook east of the Jordan, and He also had some unusual "servants" prepared to feed him. The Lord usually leads His faithful people a step at a time as they tune their hearts to His Word. God didn't give Elijah a three-year schedule to follow. Instead, He directed his servant at each critical juncture in his journey, and Elijah obeyed by faith.

"Go, hide yourself!" was God's command, and three years later the command would be, "Go, show yourself!" By leaving his public ministry, Elijah created a second "drought" in the land—an absence of the Word of the Lord. God's Word was to the Jewish people like the rain from heaven (Deut. 32:2; Isa. 55:10): it was essential to their spiritual lives, it was refreshing, and only the Lord could give it. The silence of God's servant was a judgment from God (Ps. 74:9), for not to hear God's living Word is to forfeit life itself (Ps. 28:1).

At the brook Cherith ("Kerith Ravine," NIV), Elijah had safety and sustenance. Until it dried up, the brook provided water, and each morning and evening the ravens brought him bread and meat. The raven was considered "unclean" and "detestable" on the Mosaic list of forbidden foods (Lev. 11:13-15; Deut. 14:14), yet God used these birds to help sustain the life of his servant. The ravens didn't bring Elijah the carrion that they were accustomed to eat, because such food would be unclean for a dedicated Jew. The Lord provided the food and the birds provided the transportation! Just as God dropped the manna into the camp of Israel during their wilderness journey, so He sent the necessary food to Elijah as he waited for the signal to relocate. God feeds the beasts and the ravens (Ps. 147:9; Luke 12:24), and He can use the ravens to carry food to His servant.

As the drought grew worse, the brook dried up, leaving the prophet without water; but he never made a move until the Word of the Lord came to tell him what to do. It has well been said that the will of God will never lead us where the grace of God cannot keep us and care for us, and Elijah knew this from experience. (See Isa. 33:15-16.)

3. Food from empty vessels (1 Kings 17:8-16)

Elijah lived at Cherith probably a year, and then God told him to leave. God's instructions may have shocked the prophet, for the Lord commanded him to travel northeast about a hundred miles to the Phoenician city of Zarephath. God was sending Elijah into Gentile territory, and since Zarephath was not too far from Jezebel's home city of Sidon, he would be living in enemy territory! Even more, he was instructed to live with a widow whom God had selected to care for him, and widows were usually among the neediest people in the land. Since Phoenicia depended on Israel for much of its food supply (1 Kings 5:9; Acts 12:20), food wouldn't be too plentiful there. But when God sends us, we must obey and leave the rest to Him, for we don't live on man's explanations—we live on God's promises.

"Because of our proneness to look at the bucket and forget the fountain," wrote Watchman Nee, "God has frequently to change His means of supply to keep our eyes fixed on the source." After the nation of Israel entered the Promised Land, the manna ceased to fall into the camp and God changed His way of feeding the people (Josh. 5:10-12). During the early days of the church in Jerusalem, the believers had all that they needed (Acts 4:34-35), but a few years later, the saints in Jerusalem had to receive help from the Gentile believers in Antioch (Acts 11:27-30). Elijah was about to learn what God could do with empty vessels!

The fact that the woman had been instructed by the Lord (v. 9) isn't proof that she was a believer in the God of Israel, for the Lord gave orders to a pagan king like Cyrus (2 Chron. 36:22) and even called him his "shepherd" (Isa. 44:28). The widow spoke of Jehovah as "the Lord *your* God" (v. 12, italics mine), for she could easily discern that the stranger speaking to her was a Jew; but even this isn't evidence she was a believer. It's probable that Elijah remained with her for two years (18:1), and during that time, the widow and her son surely turned from the worship of idols and put their faith in the true and living God.

The woman's assets were few: a little oil in a flask, a handful of barley in a large grain jar ("barrel", KJV), and a few sticks to provide fuel for a fire. But Elijah's assets were great, for God Almighty had promised to take care of him, his hostess, and her son. Elijah gave her God's promise that neither the jar of grain nor the flask of oil would be used up before the end of the drought and famine. God would one day send the rain, but until then, He would continue to provide bread for them—and He did.

In our modern society, with its credit cards and convenient shopping, we need to remember that each meal we eat is a miracle from the hand of God. We may live far from the farmers who grow our food, but we can't live without them. "Give us this day our daily bread" is more than a line in a prayer that we may too casually recite. It's the expression of a great truth, that the Lord cares for us and uses many hands to feed us.

> Back of the loaf is the snowy flour,
> And back of the flour is the mill,
> And back of the mill is the wheat, sun, and shower,
> The farmer—and the Father's will.

4. Life for a dead boy (1 Kings 17:17-24)

This is the first recorded instance in Scripture of the resurrection of a dead person. The evidence seems clear that the widow's son actually died and didn't just faint or go into a temporary swoon. He stopped breathing (v. 17) and his spirit left the body (vv. 21-22). According to James 2:26, when the spirit leaves a body, the person is dead. The great distress of both the mother and the prophet would suggest that the boy was dead, and both of them used the word "slay" with reference to the event (vv. 18 and 20, KJV).

The mother's response was to feel guilty because of her past sins. She believed that her son's death was God's way of punishing her for her misdeeds. It isn't unusual for people to feel guilty in connection with bereavement, but why would she point her finger at her guest? She recognized Elijah as a man of God, and perhaps she thought his presence in the home would protect her and her son from trouble. Or maybe she felt that God had informed her guest about her past life, something she should have confessed to him. Her words remind us of the question of the disciples in John 9:2, "Master, who did sin, this man, or his parents, that he was born blind?"

Elijah's response was to carry the lad to his upstairs room, perhaps on the roof, and to cry out to the Lord for the life of the child. He couldn't believe that the Lord would miraculously provide food for the three of them and then allow the son to die. It just didn't make sense. Elijah didn't stretch himself out on the boy's dead body in hopes he could transfer his life to the lad, for he knew that only God can impart life to the dead. Certainly his posture indicated total identification with the boy and his need, and this is an important factor when we intercede for others. It was after Elijah stretched himself on the child for the third time that the Lord raised him from the dead, a reminder that our own Savior arose from the dead on the third day. Because He lives, we can share His life by putting our faith in Him. (See 2 Kings 4:34 and Acts 20:10.)

The result of this miracle was the woman's public confession of her faith in the God of Israel. She now knew for sure that Elijah was a true servant of God and not just another religious teacher looking for some support. She also knew that the Word he had taught her was indeed the Word of the true and living God. During the time he lived with the widow and her son, Elijah had shown them that God sustains life (the meal and oil didn't run out) and that God imparts life (the boy was raised from the dead).

Elijah hadn't been in public ministry for a long time, yet his private ministry to the woman and her son was just as important both to the Lord and to them. The servant who won't "hide himself" and minister to a few people isn't really ready to stand on Mount Carmel and call down fire and rain from heaven. People who have proved themselves faithful with a few things in small places can be trusted by the Lord with many things before many people in the bigger places (Matt. 25:21). Elijah had proved the power of God in Baal's own home territory, so he was now ready to challenge and defeat Baal in the kingdom of Israel.

During these three years as an exile and a hunted man (18:10), Elijah has learned a great deal about the Lord, about himself and about the needs of people. He has learned to live a day at a time, trusting God for his daily bread. For three years, people have been asking, "Where is the prophet Elijah? Is he able to do anything to ease the burdens we carry because of this drought? But the Lord is more concerned about the worker than the work, and He has been preparing Elijah for the greatest challenge of faith in his entire ministry.

Before we leave the account of Elijah's sojourn with the widow of Zarephath, we must consider how our Lord used this story in the sermon He preached in the synagogue in Nazereth (Luke 4:16-30). During the first part of the sermon, the listeners approved of what Jesus said and complimented Him on His "gracious words." But then He reminded them of the sovereign grace of God that reached other nations besides the covenant people of Israel. The great Jewish prophet Elijah actually ministered to a Gentile widow and her son and had even lived with them, and yet he could have ministered to any of the many widows in the nation of Israel. His second illustration was from the ministry of Elisha, Elijah's successor, who actually healed a Gentile general of leprosy (2 Kings 5:1-15). Certainly there were plenty of Jewish lepers he might have cured!

Our Lord's emphasis was on the grace of God. He wanted the proud Jewish congregation in the synagogue to realize that the God of Israel was also the God of the Gentiles (see Rom. 3:29) and that both Jews and Gentiles were saved by putting their faith in Him. Of course, the Jews wouldn't accept the idea that they were sinners like the Gentiles and had to be saved, so they rejected both the messenger and the message and took Jesus out of the synagogue to cast Him down from the hill. Elijah's ministry to the widow and her son was proof that God is no respecter of persons and that "all have sinned and fall short of the glory of God" (Rom. 3:23). Whether a person is a religious Jew or a pagan Gentile, the only way of salvation is through faith in Jesus Christ.

5. Fire from heaven (1 Kings 18:1-40)
For three years, Elijah had hidden himself at the brook Cherith and then with the widow in Zarephath, but now he was commanded to "show himself" to wicked King Ahab. But along with God's command was God's promise that He would send rain and end the drought that He had sent to punish the idolatrous nation for over three years.

Obadiah meets Elijah (vv. 1-16). Students don't agree on the character of Obadiah, the governor of the palace. A man of great authority, he was administrator of the royal palace as well as steward and supervisor of whatever estates the king possessed. But was he a courageous servant of God (his name means "servant of Jehovah") or a timid compromiser who was afraid to let his witness be known? The text informs us that Obadiah "feared the Lord greatly" and proved it during Jezebel's "purge" by risking his life to rescue and support one hundred prophets of the Lord.[3] That doesn't sound like a man who was compromising his testimony! Why should he tell the king and queen what he was doing for the Lord? The Lord had put Obadiah in the palace to use his God-given authority to support the faithful prophets at a time when openly serving the Lord was a dangerous thing.

The king and Obadiah were searching the country for grass and other foliage that could be used to feed the horses and mules used in the army. Ahab wasn't especially concerned about the people of the land, but he wanted his army to be strong just in case of an invasion. It's remarkable that the king was willing to leave the safety and comfort of the palace to scour the land for food for the animals. It seems that when Ahab was away from Jezebel, he was a much better man.

The Lord led Elijah to the road that Obadiah was using and the two men met. Obadiah had such reverence for Elijah and his ministry that he fell on his face on the earth and called him, "My lord, Elijah." But Elijah's aim was to confront wicked King Ahab, and he wasn't about to go looking for him; so he commissioned Obadiah to tell the king where he was. We can understand Obadiah's concern lest the king come back and not find the prophet. During the three years Ahab had been searching for Elijah, no doubt he had followed up many false leads, and Ahab wasn't interested in wasting time and energy at such a critical point in the nation's history. Furthermore, Ahab might punish Obadiah or even suspect him of being a follower of Elijah's God. But when Elijah assured the officer that he would remain there and wait for the king, Obadiah went off to give Ahab the message.

Not all of God's servants are supposed to be in the public eye like Elijah and the other prophets. God has His servants in many places, doing the work He's called them to do. Nicodemus and Joseph of Arimathea didn't make a big fuss about their faith in Christ, yet God used them to give proper burial to the body of Jesus (John 19:38-42). Esther kept quiet about her Jewish heritage until it was absolutely necessary to use it to save the life of the nation. Over the centuries, there have been numerous believers who have kept a low profile and yet made great contributions to the cause of Christ and the advancement of His kingdom.

Elijah meets King Ahab (vv. 17-19). Everything that Elijah did was according to the Word of the Lord (v. 36), including confronting the king and inviting him and the priests of Baal to a meeting on Mount Carmel. Ahab called Elijah "the trouble-maker in Israel," but it was really Ahab whose sins had caused the problems in the land. Surely Ahab knew the terms of the covenant and understood that the blessings of the Lord depended on the obedience of the king and his people. Both Jesus and Paul would be called "troublemakers" (Luke 23:5; Acts 16:20; 17:6), so Elijah was in good company.

Mount Carmel was located near the border of Israel and Phoenicia, so it was a good place for the Phoenician god Baal to meet Jehovah, the God of Israel. Elijah told Ahab to bring not only the 450 prophets of Baal but also the 400 prophets of the Asherah (Astarte), the idols that represented Baal's "wife." It seems that only the prophets of Baal showed up for the contest (vv. 22, 26, 40).

The prophets of Baal meet the God of Israel (vv. 20-40). Representatives were present from all ten tribes of the Northern Kingdom, and it was this group that Elijah addressed as the meeting began. His purpose was not only to expose the false god Baal but also to bring the compromising people back to the Lord. Because of the evil influence of Ahab and Jezebel, the people were "limping" between two opinions and trying to serve both Jehovah and Baal. Like Moses (Ex. 32:26) and Joshua (Josh. 24:15) before him, Elijah called for a definite decision on their part, but the people were speechless. Was this because of their guilt (Rom. 3:19) or because they first wanted to see what would happen next? They were weak people, without true conviction.

Elijah weighted the test in favor of the prophets of Baal. They could build their altar first, select their sacrifice and offer it first, and they could take all the time they needed to pray to Baal. When Elijah said he was the only prophet of the Lord, he wasn't forgetting the prophets that Obadiah had hidden and protected. Rather, he was stating that he was the only one openly serving the Lord, and therefore he was outnumbered by the 450 prophets of Baal. But one with God is a majority, so the prophet had no fears. Surely the prayers of 450 zealous prophets would be heard by Baal and he would answer by sending fire from heaven! (See Lev. 9:24 and 1 Chron. 21:26.)

By noon, Elijah was taunting the prophets of Baal because nothing had happened. "He who sits in the heavens shall laugh; the Lord shall hold them in derision" (Ps. 2:4, NKJV). The prophets of Baal were dancing frantically around their altar and cutting themselves with swords and spears, but still nothing happened. Elijah suggested that perhaps Baal couldn't hear them because he was deep in thought, or busy in some task,[4] or even traveling. His words only made them become more fanatical, but nothing happened. At three o'clock, the time of the evening sacrifice at the temple in Jerusalem, Elijah stepped forward and took charge.

Who originally built the altar that Elijah used? Probably a member of the believing remnant in Israel who privately worshiped the Lord. But the altar had been destroyed, probably by the prophets of Baal (19:10), so Elijah rebuilt it and sanctified it. By using twelve stones, he reaffirmed the spiritual unity of God's people in spite of their political division. Elijah had given the prophets of Baal some advantages, so now he gave himself some handicaps. He had a trench dug around the altar and filled it with water. He put the sacrifice on the wood on the altar and had everything drenched with water.

At the time of the evening sacrifice, he lifted his voice in prayer to the God of the covenant, the God of Abraham, Isaac, and Jacob. His request was that God be glorified as the God of Israel, the true and living God, and make it known that Elijah was His servant. But even more, by sending fire from heaven, the Lord would be telling His people that He had forgiven them and would turn their hearts back to the worship of the true God. Elijah may have been thinking of God's promise to Solomon in 2 Chronicles 7:12-15. Suddenly, the fire fell from heaven and totally devoured the sacrifice, the altar, and the water in the trench around the altar.[5] There was nothing left that anybody could turn into a relic or a shrine. The altar to Baal still stood as a monument to a lost cause. The prophets of Baal were stunned, and the people of Israel fell on their faces and acknowledged, "The Lord, He is God!"

But Elijah wasn't yet finished, for he commanded the people to take the false prophets of Baal and slay them. This was in obedience to the Lord's command in Deuteronomy 13:13-18 and 17:2-5. The test had been a fair one and the prophets of Baal had been exposed as idolaters who deserved to be killed. The law required that idolaters be stoned to death, but Elijah had the prophets killed with the sword (19:1). This action, of course, angered Jezebel, from whose table these men had been fed (v. 19), and she determined to capture Elijah and kill him.

6. The rains return (1 Kings 18:41-45)

Elijah had announced three years before that it was his word that stopped the rain and only his word could start it again (17:1). He was referring to the power of his prayers, the words that he spoke to the Lord (James 5:17-18). It had been a long and disappointing day for King Ahab and Elijah sent him to his retainers to get something to eat.[6] Elijah went to the top of Carmel to pray and ask the Lord to send the much-needed rains. "Every day we live," wrote missionary Amy Carmichael, "we have to choose whether we should follow in the way of Ahab or of Elijah." Matthew 6:33 comes to mind.

Elijah's unusual posture was almost a fetal position and indicated the prophet's humility, his great concern for the people, and his burden for the glory of the Lord. Unlike the answer to the prayer at the altar, the answer to this prayer didn't come at once. Seven times Elijah sent his servant to look toward the Mediterranean Sea and report any indications of a storm gathering, and six of those times the servant reported nothing. The prophet didn't give up but prayed a seventh time, and the servant saw a tiny cloud coming from the sea. This is a good example for us to follow as we "watch and pray" and continue to intercede until the Lord sends the answer.

The little cloud wasn't a storm, but it was the harbinger of the rains that were to come. Elijah commanded the king to mount his chariot and return to his palace in Jezreel as soon as possible. We aren't told how he broke the news to Jezebel that Baal had been publicly humiliated and declared to be a false god, and that the prophets of Baal that she supported had been slain. But neither the drought nor the famine had brought Ahab and Jezebel to repentance, and it wasn't likely that the fire from heaven or the coming of the rain would change their hearts (Rev. 9:20-21; 16:8-11). All the evidence notwithstanding, Jezebel was determined to kill Elijah (19:1-2).

7. Strength for the journey (1 Kings 18:46)
Soon the heavens were black with clouds and great torrents of rain began to fall on the land. The Lord not only proved that he was the true and living God, but He also put His approval on the ministry of His servant Elijah. Elijah had neither chariots nor retainers to drive them, but he did have the power of the Lord; and he ran ahead of Ahab and reached Jezreel ahead of the king, a distance of about seventeen miles. This was quite a feat for an older man and in itself was another sign to the people that God's powerful hand was upon His servant.

God had chastened His people with drought and famine but had cared for His special servant Elijah. God had sent fire from heaven to prove that He was the true and living God. Now He had answered the prayer of His prophet and had sent the rains to water the land. You would think that Elijah would be at his very best spiritually and able to face anything, but the next chapter records just the opposite. As great a man as Elijah was, he still failed the Lord and himself.

The Cave Man

It encourages me when I read James 5:17, "Elijah was as human as we are" (NLT). I have a tendency to idealize the men and women in Scripture, but the Bible is the "word of truth" (2 Tim. 2:15) and describes the warts and wrinkles of even the greatest. When James wrote those words, he undoubtedly had 1 Kings 18 and 19 in mind, for in these chapters we see Elijah at his highest and at his lowest. When the psalmist wrote that "every man at his best state is altogether vanity" (Ps. 39:5, KJV), he included all of us except Jesus. An old adage reminds us, "The best of men are but men at their best," and Elijah's history proves how true this is.

However, the outstanding leaders in Scripture, with all their humanness, knew how to find their way out of what John Bunyan called "the slough [swamp] of despond" and get back on track with the Lord. We can learn from their defeats as well as their successes. Furthermore, by studying passages like 1 Kings 19, we're reminded to give glory to the Master and not to His servants (1 Cor. 1:27-29). We're also reminded to prepare for what may happen after the victories God gives us. How quickly we can move from the mountaintop of triumph to the valley of testing! We need to humble ourselves before the Lord and get ready for the trials that usually follow the victories.

If Elijah could have described to a counselor how he felt and what he thought, the counselor would have diagnosed his condition as a textbook case of burnout. Elijah was physically exhausted and had lost his appetite. He was depressed about himself and his work and was being controlled more and more by self-pity. "I only am left!" Instead of turning to others for help, he isolated himself and—worst of all—he wanted to die. (Elijah never did die. He was taken to heaven in a chariot. See 2 Kings 2.) The prophet concluded that he had failed in his mission and decided it was time to quit. But the Lord didn't see it that way. He always looks beyond our changing moods and impetuous prayers, and He pities us the way parents pity their discouraged children (Ps. 103:13-14). The chapter shows us how tenderly and patiently God deals with us when we're in the depths of despair and feel like giving up.

The chapter begins with Elijah running away and trying to save himself. Then the prophet argues with the Lord and tries to defend himself. Finally, he obeys the Lord and yields himself and is restored to service. In all of this, Elijah was responding to four different messages.

1. The enemy's message of danger (1 Kings 19:1-4)

When the torrential rain began to fall, Jezebel was in Jezreel and may have thought that Baal the storm god had triumphed on Mount Carmel. However, when Ahab arrived home, he told her a much different story. Ahab was a weak man, but he should have stood with Elijah and honored the Lord who had so dramatically demonstrated His power. But Ahab had to live with Queen Jezebel and without her support, he knew he was nothing. If ever there was a strong-willed ruler with a gift for doing evil, it was Jezebel. Neither Ahab nor Jezebel accepted the clear evidence given on Mount Carmel that Jehovah was the only true and living God. Instead of repenting and calling the nation back to serving the Lord, Jezebel declared war on Jehovah and His faithful servant Elijah, and Ahab allowed her to do it.

Why did Jezebel send a letter to Elijah when she could have

sent soldiers and had him killed? He was in Jezreel and the deed could have been easily accomplished on such a wild and stormy night. Jezebel wasn't only an evil woman; she was also a shrewd strategist who knew how to make the most of Baal's defeat on Mount Carmel. Ahab was a quitter, but not his wife! Elijah was now a very popular man. Like Moses, he had brought fire from heaven, and like Moses, he had slain the idolaters (Lev. 9:24; Num. 25). If Jezebel transformed the prophet into a martyr, he might influence people more by his death than by his life. No, the people were waiting for Elijah to tell them what to do, so why not *remove him from the scene of his victory?* If Elijah disappeared, the people would wonder what had happened, and they would be prone to drift back into worshiping Baal and letting Ahab and Jezebel have their way. Furthermore, whether from Baal or Jehovah, the rains had returned and there was work to do!

Jezebel may have suspected that Elijah was a candidate for a physical and emotional breakdown after his demanding day on Mount Carmel, and she was right. He was as human as we are, and as the ancient church fathers used to say to their disciples, "Beware of human reactions after holy exertions." Her letter achieved its purpose and Elijah fled from Jezreel. In a moment of fear,[1] when he forgot all that God had done for him the previous three years, Elijah took his servant, left Israel, and headed for Beersheba, the southernmost city in Judah. Charles Spurgeon said that Elijah "retreated before a beaten enemy." God had answered his prayer (18:36-37) and God's hand had been upon him in the storm (18:46), but now he was walking by sight and not by faith. (See Ps. 16:7-8.)

For three years, Elijah had not made a move without hearing and obeying the Lord's instructions (17:2-3, 8-9; 18:1), but now he was running ahead of the Lord in order to save his own life. When God's servants get out of God's will, they're liable to do all sorts of foolish things *and fail in their strongest points.* When Abraham fled to Egypt, he failed in his faith, which was his greatest strength (Gen. 12:10ff). David's greatest strength was his integrity, and that's where he failed when he started lying and scheming during the Bathsheba episode (2 Sam. 11–12). Moses was the meekest of men (Num. 12:3), yet he lost his temper and forfeited the privilege of entering the Promised Land (Num. 20:1-13). Peter was a courageous man, yet his courage failed and he denied Christ (Mark 14:66-72). Like Peter, Elijah was a bold man, but his courage failed when he heard Jezebel's message.

But why flee to Judah, especially when Jehoram, king of Judah was married to Ahab's daughter Athaliah (2 Kings 8:16-19; 2 Chron. 21:4-7). This is the infamous Athaliah who later ruled the land and tried to exterminate all of David's heirs to the throne (2 Kings 11). The safest place for any child of God is the place dictated by the will of God, but Elijah didn't stop to seek God's will. He traveled 90 to 100 miles to Beersheba and left his servant there. Did he say, "Stay here until I return?" or did he just set the man free for his own safety. If the enemy came after Elijah, his servant would be safer someplace else. Furthermore, if the servant didn't know where Elijah was, he couldn't inform against him.

Beersheba had a special meaning to the Jews because of its associations with Abraham (Gen. 21:22, 33), Isaac (26:33), and Jacob (46:1). The "juniper tree"[2] is actually a flowering shrub ("the flowering broom tree") that flourishes in the wilderness and provides shade for flocks and herds and travelers. The branches are thin and supple like those of the willow and are used to bind bundles. (The Hebrew word for this shrub means "to bind.") The roots of the plant are used for fuel and make excellent charcoal (Ps. 120:4). As Elijah sat under its shade, he did a wise thing—he prayed—but did didn't pray a very wise prayer. "I've had enough!" he told the Lord, "so take my life."[3] Then he gave his reason: "I'm no better than my fathers." But God never asked him to be better than anybody else, but only to hear His Word and obey it.

The combination of emotional burnout, weariness, hunger, and a deep sense of failure, plus lack of faith in the Lord, had brought Elijah into deep depression. But there was also an element of pride involved, and also some self-pity, for Elijah was sure that his courageous ministry on Mount Carmel would bring the nation to its knees. Perhaps he was also hoping that Ahab and Jezebel would repent and turn from Baal to Jehovah. His expectations weren't fulfilled, so he considered himself a failure. But the Lord rarely allows His servants to see all the good they have done, because we walk by faith and not by sight, and Elijah would learn that there were 7,000 people in Israel who had not bowed to Baal and worshiped him. No doubt his own ministry had influenced many of them.

2. The angel's message of grace (1 Kings 19:5-8)

When the heart is heavy and the mind and body are weary, some-times the best remedy is sleep—just take a nap! Referring to Mark 6:31, Vance Havner used to say that if we didn't come apart and rest, we'd come apart—and Elijah was about to come apart. Nothing seems right when you're exhausted.

But while the prophet was asleep, the Lord sent an angel to care for his needs. In both Hebrew and Greek, the word translat-ed "angel" also means "messenger," so some have concluded that this helpful visitor was another traveler whom the Lord brought to Elijah's side just at the right time. However, in verse 7, the vis-itor is called "the angel of the Lord," an Old Testament title for the second Person of the Godhead, Jesus Christ, the Son of God. In passages like Genesis 16:10, Exodus 3:1-4 and Judges 2:1-4, the angel of the Lord speaks and acts as God would speak and act. In fact the angel of the Lord in Exodus 3:2 is called "God" and "the Lord" in the rest of the chapter. We assume that this help-ful visitor was our Lord Jesus Christ.

Elijah and the Apostle Peter were both awakened by angels (Acts 12:7), Elijah to get some nourishment and Peter to walk out a free man. The angel had prepared a simple but adequate meal of fresh bread and refreshing water, and the prophet partook of both and lay down again to sleep. (Jesus prepared a breakfast of bread and fish for Peter and six other of His disciples; John 21:9, 13.) We aren't told how long the Lord permitted Elijah to sleep before He awakened him the second time and told him to eat. The Lord knew that Elijah planned to visit Mount Sinai, one of the most sacred places in all Jewish history, and Sinai was located about 250 miles from Beersheba, and he needed strength for the journey. But no matter what our destination may be, the journey is too great for us and we need God's strength to reach the goal. How gracious God was to spread a "table in the wilderness" for His discouraged servant (Ps. 78:19, and see Ps. 23:5). Elijah obeyed the messenger of God and was able to travel for forty days and nights on the nourishment from those two meals.

When you review God's ministries to Elijah as recorded in 1 Kings 18 and 19, you see a parallel to the promise in Isaiah 40:31. For three years, the prophet had been hidden by God, during which time he "waited on the Lord." When the Lord sent him to Mount Carmel, He enabled Elijah to "mount up with wings as eagles" and triumph over the prophets of Baal. After Elijah prayed and it began to rain, the Lord strengthened him to "run and not be weary" (18:46), and now He sustained him for forty days so he could "walk and not faint" (19:8). Elijah wasn't wholly living in the will of God, but he was smart enough to know that he had to wait on the Lord if he expected to have strength for the ministry and for the journey that lay before him.

God's angels are His special ambassadors, sent to minister to His people (Heb. 1:14; Ps. 91:11). An angel rescued Daniel from being devoured by lions (Dan. 6:22), and angels attended Jesus during His temptation in the wilderness (Mark 1:12-13). An angel strengthened Jesus in the Garden of Gethsemane (Luke 22:43) and encouraged Paul on board ship in the storm (Acts 27:23). The angels in heaven rejoice when a sinner is converted (Luke 15:7, 10). When we arrive in heaven and God privileges us to review our earthly walk, we will no doubt discover that strangers who helped us in different ways were actually the angels of God, sent by the Lord to assist and protect us.

3. The Creator's message of power (1 Kings 19:9-14)

It was about 200 miles from Beersheba to Sinai, a journey of perhaps ten days to two weeks. It had been three weeks at the most since Elijah fled from Jezreel, but the trip expanded to consume forty days (19:8)! If Elijah was in such a hurry to put miles between himself and Jezebel's executioners, why did he take such a long time to do it? Perhaps the Lord directed his steps (Ps. 37:23) —and his stops—so that he would spend one day for every year the Israelites had been in the wilderness after they were delivered from Egypt. It was Israel's unbelief and fear at Kadesh Barnea that led to their judgment (Num. 13–14), and it was Elijah's unbelief and fear that led to his journeying in the desert. (Our Lord also spent forty days in the wilderness when He was tempted; Matt. 4:2.) Since he was heading for Sinai, Elijah may have planned the trip so he could spend forty days in the wilderness to imitate Moses who spent forty days on the mount with the Lord (Ex. 34:28). Elijah had to deal with Baal worship and Moses had to deal with the worship of the golden calf (Ex. 32).[4]

Elijah made the cave his home and waited upon the Lord. In contemporary religious language, he was "making a retreat" in order to solve some problems and get closer to the Lord. He was so depressed that he was willing to give up his calling and even his life. When the Lord finally came and spoke to Elijah, it wasn't to rebuke him or instruct him but to ask him a question: "What are you doing here?" The prophet's reply didn't really answer the question, which explains why God asked it a second time (v. 13). Elijah only told the Lord (who already knew) that he had experienced many trials in his ministry, but he had been faithful to the Lord. But if he was a faithful servant, what was he doing hiding in a cave located hundreds of miles from his appointed place of ministry?

In this reply, Elijah reveals both pride and self-pity, and in using the pronoun "they," he exaggerates the size of the opposition. He makes it look as though every last Jew in the Northern Kingdom had turned against him and the Lord, when actually it was Jezebel who wanted to kill him. The "I only am left" refrain[5] makes it look as though he was indispensable to God's work, when actually no servant of God is indispensable. God then commanded him to stand on the mount at the entrance of the cave, but it doesn't appear that Elijah obeyed him until he heard the still small voice (v. 13). Another possibility is that he did go out of the cave but fled back into it when God began to demonstrate His great power.

"The Lord passed by" reminds us of the experience of Moses on the mount (Ex. 33:21-22). All Elijah needed to get renewed for service was a fresh vision of the power and glory of God. First, the Lord caused a great wind to pass by, a wind so strong that it broke the rocks and tore the mountain, but no divine message came to the prophet. Then the Lord caused a great earthquake that shook the mount, but nothing from God came out of the earthquake. The Lord then brought a fire, but it too gave Elijah no message from the Lord. Certainly the prophet must have thought of the giving of the law as he witnessed this dramatic display of power (Ex. 19:16-18).

What was God trying to accomplish in Elijah's life by means of these awesome and frightening object lessons? For one thing, He was reminding His servant that everything in nature was obedient to Him (Ps. 148)—the wind, the foundations of the earth, the fire—and He didn't lack for a variety of tools to get His work done. If Elijah wanted to resign from his divine calling, the Lord had someone else to take his place. As it turned out, Elijah didn't resign but was given the privilege of calling his successor Elisha and spending time with him before being taken to heaven.

The wind, the earthquake, and the fire are all means that the Lord has used to manifest Himself to mankind. Theologians call these demonstrations "theophanies," from two Greek words (*theos* = God; *phaino* = to manifest, to appear) that together mean "the manifestation of God." The pagan nations saw these great sights and worshipped the powers of nature, but when the Jews saw them, they worshiped the God who created nature. (See Jud. 5:4-5, Ps.18:16-18 and Hab. 3.) But these same demonstrations of the awesome presence and power of God will be seen in the last days before Jesus returns to earth to establish His kingdom. The Old Testament prophets called this period "the day of the Lord." (See Joel 2:28-3:16, Isa. 13:9-10, Matt. 24:29, and Rev. 6-16.) Perhaps the Lord was saying to Elijah, "You feel like you've failed to judge the sin in Israel, but one day I will judge it and my judgment is final and complete."

After this dramatic display of power, there was "a still small voice," which has also been translated "a gentle whisper, a tone of a gentle blowing." When the prophet heard that voice, he stepped out of the cave and met the Lord. The mighty power and the great noise of the previous exhibitions didn't stir Elijah, but when he heard the still small voice, he recognized the voice of God. For the second time (see Jonah 3:1), he heard the same question, "What are you doing here, Elijah?" and once again, Elijah repeated the same self-centered evasive answer.

God was saying to Elijah, "You called fire from heaven, you had the prophets of Baal slain, and you prayed down a terrific rainstorm, but now you feel like a failure. But you must realize that I don't usually work in a manner that's loud, impressive, and dramatic. My still small voice brings the Word to the listening ear and heart. Yes, there's a time and place for the wind, the earthquake and the fire, but most of the time, I speak to people in tones of gentle love and quiet persuasion." The Lord wasn't condemning the courageous ministry of His servant; He was only reminding Elijah that He uses many different tools to accomplish His work. God's Word comes down like the gentle shower that refreshes, cleanses, and produces life (Deut. 32:2; Isa. 55:10).

In this day of mammoth meetings, loud music, and high-pressure promotion, it's difficult for some people to understand that God rarely works by means of the dramatic and the colossal. When He wanted to start the Jewish nation, He sent a baby— Isaac; and when He wanted to deliver that nation from bondage, He sent another baby—Moses. He sent a teenager named David to kill the Philistine giant, and the boy used a sling and a stone to do it. When God wanted to save a world, He sent His Son as a weak and helpless baby; and today, God seeks to reach that world through the ministry of "earthen vessels" (2 Cor. 4:7, KJV). Dr. J. Oswald Sanders states that "the whispers from Calvary are infinitely more potent than the thunder of Sinai in bringing men to repentance."[6]

4. The Lord's message of hope (1 Kings 19:15-21)

Elijah had nothing new to say to the Lord, but the Lord had a new message of hope for His frustrated servant. The Lord had many reasons for rejecting His servant and leaving him to die in the cave, but He didn't take that approach. "He has not dealt with us according to our sins, nor punished us according to our iniquities. . . . For He knows our frame; He remembers that we are dust" (Ps. 103:10, 14, NKJV).

First, the Lord told Elijah to return to the place of duty. When we're out of the Lord's will, we have to retrace our steps and make a new beginning (Gen. 13:3; 35:1-3). The honest answer to the question "What are you doing here, Elijah?" was "Nothing! I'm have a personal pity party!" But Elijah was called to serve, and there were tasks to perform. When Joshua was brokenhearted because of Israel's defeat at Ai, he spent a day on his face before God; but God's answer was, "Get up! Why do you lie thus on your face?" (Josh. 7:10, NKJV). When Samuel mourned over the failure of Saul, God rebuked him. "How long will you mourn for Saul, seeing I have rejected him from reigning over Israel? Fill your horn with oil, and go . . . " (1 Sam. 16:1, NKJV); and Samuel went and anointed David to be the next king. *No matter how much or how often His servants fail Him, God is never at a loss to know what to do.* Our job is to obey His Word and get up and do it!

Elijah's first responsibility was to anoint Hazael to be king of Syria. This was a Gentile nation, but it was still the Lord who chose the leaders. "[The] Most High rules in the kingdom of men, and gives it to whomever He chooses" (Dan. 4:25, NKJV). Then he was to anoint Jehu to be king of Israel, for even though the nation had divided, Israel was still under the divine covenant and was responsible to the Lord. His third task was to anoint Elisha to be his own successor. Elijah had complained because the past generation had failed and the present generation hadn't done any better (v. 4). Now God called him to help equip the future generation by anointing two kings and a prophet.[7] This is the Old Testament version of 2 Timothy 2:2.

The people the Lord named weren't especially significant in the social structure of that day. Hazael was a servant to King Bedhadad, Jehu was a captain of the army, and Elisha was a farmer. But by the time Elisha and Jehu completed their work, Baal worship was almost wiped out in Israel (2 Kings 10:18-31). No one generation can do everything, but each generation must see to it that people in the next generation are called and trained and that the tools are made available for them to continue the work of the Lord. God was calling Elijah to stop weeping over the past and running away from the present. It was time for him to start preparing others for the future. When God is in command, there is always hope.

But the Lord did more than send His servant out to recruit new workers. He also gave him the assurance that his work and their work would not be in vain. God would use the swords of Hazael and Jehu, and the words and works of Elisha, to accomplish His purposes in the land. Even more, He assured Elijah that his own ministry hadn't been a failure for there were still 7,000 people in the land who were faithful to Jehovah. Indeed, the prophet was not alone, *yet God sent him to touch the lives of three individuals*. The Lord didn't command Elijah to gather all 7,000 faithful people together in a mass meeting and preach a sermon. There's certainly a place for sermons and large meetings, but we must never underestimate the importance of working with individuals. Jesus spoke to huge crowds, but He always had time for individuals and their needs.

The phrase "I have left" in verse 18 (KJV) means "I have reserved for myself." This is "the remnant according to the election of grace" that Paul wrote about in Romans 11:1-6. No matter how wicked the world scene may appear, God always has a remnant that is faithful to Him. Sometimes that remnant is small, but God is always great and accomplishes His purposes.

Without delay, Elijah retraced his steps and returned to the place of duty. It was 150 miles from Sinai to Abel Meholah (v. 16) where he would find Elisha plowing a field. Elisha's name means "God has salvation." The fact that Elisha was using twelve yoke of oxen—twenty-four expensive animals—indicates that his family was probably better off financially than most Israelites.[8] Elijah didn't say a word to the young man but merely cast his mantle (outer garment) over him to indicate that the Lord had called him to serve the prophet and then be his successor. Elisha and his family were part of that "remnant of grace" that God had set apart for Himself. No matter how bleak the days may seem, God has His people and knows when to call them.

Elisha's conduct seems to contradict what Jesus said in Luke 9:57-62, but this is not so. Elisha was wholehearted in his obedience to follow after Elijah, while the men in the Gospel record had hesitations and reservations, and Jesus knew it. Elisha proved his commitment by killing two of the oxen and using the wooden farm implements as fuel to cook them for a farewell feast. In contemporary terms, he was "burning his bridges behind him." He had no intention of taking his hand off the plow and then going back to it. Elijah's reply means, "What have I done? I didn't call you, the Lord did. Am I stopping you? Do as the Lord wants you to do." The *New Living Translation* reads, "Go on back! But consider what I have done to you." How Elisha's family and friends viewed this sudden change of vocation isn't shared with us, but there's no indication they were opposed to Elisha's decision.

As you review the chapter, you can see the mistakes that Elijah made and how the Lord overruled them and accomplished His will. Elijah walked by sight and not by faith, yet the Lord sustained him. He looked at himself and his failures instead of at God's greatness and power. He was more concerned about doing more than his ancestors had done in the past instead of calling and preparing new servants for the future. He isolated himself from God's people and thereby lost the strength and encouragement of their fellowship and prayers. But let's not be too hard on Elijah, for he did have a sensitive ear to the still small voice of the Lord, and he did obey what God told him to do. The Lord rebuked him gently and brought him out of his cave and back into active service. Let's keep these things in mind and recall them the next time we're under our juniper tree or in our cave!

Finally, let's be among those who look to the future and seek to enlist others to serve the Lord. To glamorize or criticize the past accomplishes little; what's important is that we do our job in the present and equip others to continue it after we're gone. God buried His workers, but His work goes right on.

TWELVE

Ahab, *the Slave of Sin*

In his novel *Moby-Dick,* Herman Melville gave the name Ahab to the deranged captain of the whaling vessel *Pequod.* (Melville also included a "prophet" named Elijah.) The Ahab in the Bible is a weak man who destroyed himself and his family because he allowed his evil wife Jezebel to turn him into a monster. The name Jezebel is familiar to people today and has even made it into the dictionary: "Jezebel—an evil, shameless woman." To call a woman "a Jezebel" is to put her on the lowest level of society (see Rev. 2:20-23). The prophet Elijah described the man accurately when he told Ahab, "I have found you, because you have sold yourself to do evil in the sight of the Lord" (1 Kings 21:20, NKJV).

These chapters describe four events in Ahab's life: three battles with the Syrians (Aram) and a land-grab scam that involved an illegal trial and several murders. Because he wasn't rightly related to the Lord and His Word, Ahab was enslaved to sin, but "the wages of sin is death" (Rom. 6:23), and Ahab received his wages with dividends. We will look at the four events and see Ahab's varied responses.

1. Believing God's promise (1 Kings 20:1-30)

This is the first of two occasions when wicked King Ahab showed a glimmer of spiritual understanding. Israel was just coming out three years of famine when Ben-hadad, King of Syria, decided to attack and take advantage of their plight. King David had defeated these northern nations (called Syria in the older translations, Aram in the newer ones), but these nations had gradually regained their independence. Another factor in Ben-hadad's attack was the growing strength of Assyria in the north. Ben-hadad wanted to control the trade routes through Israel because he had lost the northern routes to Assyria, and he also wanted to be sure that Israel would provide men and weapons in case of an Assyrian invasion.

The siege (20:1-12). The thirty-two "kings" who allied with Ben-hadad were the rulers of northern city-states whose safety and prosperity depended a good deal on the strength of Syria. We aren't told how long the siege of Samaria lasted, but Syria ultimately brought Ahab to the place of submission. First, Ben-hadad demanded Ahab's wealth and family, and Ahab agreed. Ben-hadad planned to hold the family hostage just to make sure Ahab didn't back out of his agreement. Instead of Ahab calling for Elijah or another prophet and seeking the help of the Lord, he quickly capitulated. (Contrast this decision with Saul's decision in 1 Samuel 11.) Ben-hadad wasn't satisfied with this arrangement and wanted more, but his covetousness led to his defeat. In addition to taking the king's wealth and the royal family, Ben-hadad wanted to send officers to search all the royal buildings and take whatever they wanted! Agreeing with this request was much too humiliating for proud Ahab, so he and his advisers refused to accept it.

When he received Ahab's message, Ben-hadad was probably drunk and feeling very brave, because he made an unwise decision. He could have gotten most of what he wanted without sacrificing a single soldier, but now he made an oath to grind Samaria to powder, and he had to live up to his boast. To his credit, Ahab replied with a familiar proverb that could have applied to him as much as to Ben-hadad. It's the equivalent of, "Don't count your chickens before they hatch."

The promise (20:13-21). In opposing Ben-hadad, Ahab had nothing to stand on, but God in His grace sent him a message of hope: the Lord would give Ahab the victory. The Lord wasn't doing this because Ahab deserved it but because He wanted to honor His own name before the wavering king of Israel and his people. As He did on Mount Carmel, so Jehovah would do on the battlefield: He would demonstrate that He alone is God (18:36-37). We commend Ahab for receiving the promise and asking for further instructions. Perhaps Jezebel wasn't home that day to influence him the wrong way.

Following the example of Solomon (1 Kings 4:7ff), Ahab's father Omri had divided the kingdom of Israel into a number of political districts, each in charge of a "provincial leader" who was also an army officer. The Lord selected these leaders to lead the attack against Syria, and Ahab was to lead the small army of 7,000 men. They went out at noon, knowing that Ben-hadad and his officers would be eating and drinking and be in no condition to fight a battle. Even when Ben-hadad's scouts reported that a company of men was approaching the Syrian camp, the Syrian king wasn't afraid but told the guard to take them alive. The military strategy for capturing prisoners would be different from that for destroying an invading army, so Ahab's men caught the Syrian guards by surprise and proceeded to wipe out the Syrian army. Instead of measuring the dust of Samaria as he threatened (v. 10), Ben-hadad jumped on his horse and escaped with his life. But because Ahab believed God's Word and acted upon it, God gave him a great victory.

The challenge (20:22-30). Another anonymous prophet spoke to Ahab and cautioned him to strengthen his forces and be prepared for another invasion. While Ahab was listening to God's message, Ben-hadad was listening to his officers explain Syria's great defeat. They were healing their king's wounded pride while at the same time protecting their own lives. They explained that their great army wasn't at fault; the defeat was the fault of the terrain. The gods of the Syrians were "gods of the plains," while Israel's God was a "god of the hills." Change the location and Syria will have the victory.

We now have a different scenario, because not only was the enemy challenging God's people, *he was challenging God Himself!* This was the Mount Carmel contest all over again, and the Lord wouldn't let it go unchallenged. Jehovah is the Lord of all the earth! He sent another man of God to assure Ahab of victory, but only because He wanted Ahab, the army of Israel, and the men of Syria to know that Jehovah alone is God. The Lord gave Israel victory on the battlefield, and when the enemy fled into the city of Aphek, God sent an earthquake and killed 27,000 Syrian soldiers.[1] By the grace of God, Ahab won a second great victory!

2. Disobeying God's command (1 Kings 20:31-43)
When God sent King Saul to fight the Amalekites, He made it clear that He wanted the Israelites to completely destroy them (1 Sam. 15). Saul disobeyed the Lord and as a result lost his kingdom. The Lord must have given a similar command to King Ahab (v. 42), but he too disobeyed. Ahab won the battle but lost the victory. What the enemy couldn't accomplish with their weapons, they accomplished with their deception. If Satan can't succeed as the lion who devours (1 Peter 5:8), he will come as a serpent to deceives (2 Cor. 11:3). Even Joshua fell into a similar trap (Josh. 9).

Ben-hadad's officers were clever men who knew it was worth the risk to appeal to Ahab's pride. God had given the victory but Ahab would take the credit and claim the spoils. In their dress and their attitude, the officers pretended to show humble submission to Ahab as he waited in his chariot (v. 33). Ahab certainly enjoyed the "honor" he was receiving after the great victory, but not once did he give the glory to the Lord. To hear that Ben-hadad was his servant made his heart glad, and he was more than willing to spare the man's life. Later, Hazael would kill Ben-hadad and become the king (2 Kings 8).

Ben-hadad immediately entered into a treaty with Ahab and

gave back to Israel the cities his father had taken (1 Kings 15:20). He also gave Ahab permission to sell Israel's produce and wares in the market at Damascus, which amounted to a trade agreement. That the king of Israel should make such a treaty with the enemy is remarkable, but Ahab had no convictions (except those of his wife) and always took the easy way out of any situation. Furthermore, he needed the support of Aram in case the Assyrians should decide to move south. This treaty lasted three years (22:1).

The Lord couldn't allow Ahab to disobey and get away with it, so He instructed one of the sons of the prophets to confront the king about his sin. The "sons of the prophets" were young men who had special prophetic gifts and met in groups to study with elder prophets like Samuel (1 Sam. 7:17; 28:3), Elijah, and Elisha (2 Kings 2:3-7, 16; 4:38, 40). Knowing that he would have to catch Ahab by surprise to get his attention, the man wisely set up an "action sermon" that would arouse the king's interest.[2] The young man told a fellow student about God's orders and asked him to strike him with a weapon, but the man refused. We can understand a friend not wanted to injure a friend, but like Ahab, the young prophet was disobeying God, and it cost him his life. This certainly put the fear of God into the other students, because the next one the young man approached was only too willing to comply. Disguised as a wounded soldier, he was ready to deliver his message.[3]

In those days, a person could approach the king to help decide matters that needed legal clarification; and when Ahab saw this "injured soldier" sitting by the side of the road, his curiosity was aroused. Now we have a replay of Nathan's approach to David after David committed adultery with Bathsheba (2 Sam. 12), for just as David determined his own sentence, so Ahab announced his own guilt! Hearing that the "soldier" had lost an important prisoner of war and would have to forfeit his life or pay an enormous fine (75 pounds of silver), the king replied, "So shall your judgment be; you yourself have decided it" (v. 40, NASB). The king could have granted the man a pardon and saved his life, but he preferred to let him die. *But in so doing, Ahab was declaring his own guilt and passing sentence on himself!*

How did Ahab recognize that the young man was one of the sons of the prophets? It's not likely that Ahab was that close to Elijah's followers to know them personally. When the bandage was removed, did it reveal some identifying mark? Had Ahab seen the man on Mount Carmel? We have no way of knowing, but the sight must have shocked the king. The man that Ahab judged now became Ahab's judge and announced that one day the Syrians would slay Ahab. But instead of repenting and seeking the Lord's forgiveness, Ahab went home and pouted like a child (v. 43; see 21:4).

3. Breaking God's laws (1 Kings 21:1-16)

Ben-hadad was the man Ahab should have killed, but he set him free; and Naboth was the man Ahab should have protected, but Ahab killed him! When you sell yourself to do evil, you call evil good and good evil, light darkness and darkness light (Isa. 5:20). The infamous episode of Naboth's vineyard reveals the lawlessness of King Ahab and his evil wife Jezebel. Consider the sins they committed and consequently the commandments of God that they disdained and disobeyed.

Idolatry. The first two commandments in the Decalogue declare that the Lord is the only true God and that true worshipers do not worship and serve other gods, whether things in God's creation or things they make themselves (Ex. 20:1-6). "The essence of idolatry is the entertainment of thoughts about God that are unworthy of Him," wrote A. W. Tozer.[4] Jezebel brought Baal worship into Israel and Ahab permitted it to spread throughout the land. When you turn away from truth, it's evidence that you're believing lies, then you start loving lies, and before long, you're controlled by lies.

Covetousness (vv. 1-4). Ahab and Jezebel had a summer palace at Jezreel, but the king couldn't enjoy it fully without a vegetable garden. Powerful people acquire one thing after another, but in all their acquiring, there's never any real satisfaction. "A man is rich in proportion to the number of things he can afford to let alone," wrote Henry David Thoreau in chapter two of *Walden*. Then he added later in the book, "Superfluous wealth can buy superfluities only. Money is not required to buy one necessity of the soul."

The king wanted Naboth's vineyard because he coveted a garden convenient to the palace.

"Thou shalt not covet" is the last of the Ten Commandments (Ex. 20:17) but perhaps it's the most difficult one to obey. Even more, a covetous heart often leads us to disobey all the other commandments of God. The first nine Commandments focus on forbidden outward conduct—making and worshiping idols, stealing, murdering, and so on—but this commandment deals primarily with the hidden desires of the heart. It was the Tenth Commandment that helped Saul of Tarsus, the Pharisee, realize what he sinner he really was (Rom. 7:7-25); and it was this commandment that the wealthy young ruler refused to acknowledge when he looked into the mirror of the law (Matt. 19:14-30).

Ahab masked his covetousness by first offering to buy the vineyard or trade it for another piece of property. It was a reasonable offer, but Naboth was more concerned about obeying God's Word than pleasing the king or even making money. Naboth knew that the land belonged to the Lord and that He loaned it to the people of Israel to enjoy as long as they obeyed His covenant. All property had to be kept in the family (Lev. 25:23-28), which meant that Naboth was forbidden to sell his land to the king. Displaying his usual childishness, Ahab went home, went to bed, and pouted.

False witness (vv. 5-10). "Thou shalt not bear false witness against thy neighbor" is the ninth commandment and emphasizes the important of speaking the truth, whether in court or over the back fence. Truth is the cement that holds society together, and when truth is gone, everything starts to fall apart (Isa. 59:14). Jezebal was a resolute woman who never allowed the truth to stand in the way of what she wanted, so she fabricated an official lie, on official stationery, sealed with the official seal.

But no amount of royal adornment could change the fact that Ahab and Jezebel were breaking God's law.

What right did Jezebel have to write Naboth's death warrant? He husband was king! Since she came from Phoenicia, she had the Gentile view of kingship, which included being important, getting what you want and using your authority to take care of yourself. Samuel warned about this kind of monarch (1 Sam. 8:14), and Jesus cautioned His disciples not to follow that philosophy of governing but to serve the people in love (Matt. 20:20-28). A true leader uses his authority to build the people, while a dictator uses the people to build his authority, and people are expendable. Jezebel even threw in some religion and told the local authorities to proclaim a fast. If you can sugarcoat your scheme with something religious, the people will quickly accept it. But no matter how legal and spiritual that royal edict may have looked, in the sight of God it was only a lie—and God judges liars. Everything that God hates, Ahab and Jezebel did (Prov. 6:16-19).

Murder (vv. 11-13). The procedure Jezebel outlined was in agreement with the law (Deut. 17:6-7; 19:15; Num. 35:30), but the accusation was false, the witnesses were liars, and the judges had been bought off by royal intimidation. In every town there were "men of Belial—worthless fellows" who would do anything for money or just to become important. Nobody but Ahab and possibly Jezebel heard Naboth's refusal to sell, and there was nothing in his words that could be interpreted as blasphemy. To curse God was a capital crime (Lev. 24:13-16), and cursing the king was dangerous because he was God's appointed ruler (Ex. 22:28; Acts 23:5).[5]

Stealing (vv. 14-16). The weak rulers in Naboth's city followed Jezebel's orders, conducted their illegal trial, took Naboth and his sons (2 Kings 9:26) outside the city, and stoned them. Nobody in the family was alive who could inherit the land, so Ahab felt he was free to take it. The officers notified Jezebel, not Ahab, of the execution, so it's obvious who had the power in the royal family. But the land didn't belong to Ahab, and the law says, "Thou shalt not steal" (Ex. 20:15, KJV). The vineyard hadn't even belonged to Naboth—it belonged to the Lord. Ahab was stealing property from God!

If ever two people were guilty of blaspheming God and breaking His laws, it was Ahab and Jezebel, and judgment was about to fall.

4. Hearing God's sentence (1 Kings 21:16-29)

"Surely the Lord does nothing, unless He reveals His secret to His servants the prophets" (Amos 3:7, NKJV). We have heard nothing from or about Elijah since he called Elisha to be his successor, but now God brings His servant into center stage to confront the king. As He always does when he gives an assignment, He told Elijah just what to say to the evil king. Ahab had shed innocent blood and his guilty blood would be licked up by the dogs. What a way for the king of Israel to end his reign!

Previously, Ahab called Elijah "the troubler of Israel" (18:17), but now he makes it more personal and calls the prophet "my enemy." Actually, by fighting against the Lord, Ahab was his own enemy and brought upon himself the sentence that Elijah pronounced. Ahab would die dishonorably and the dogs would lick his blood. Jezebel would die and be eaten by the dogs. All of their posterity would eventually be eradicated from the land. They had enjoyed their years of sinful pleasure and selfish pursuits, but it would all end in judgment.

Instead of going home to pout, Ahab actually repented! What his wife thought about his actions isn't recorded, but the Lord who sees the heart accepted his humiliation and told it to His servant. The Lord didn't cancel the announced judgments but postponed them until the reign of Ahab's son Joram. See 2 Kings 9:14-37. Ahab was slain on the battlefield and the dogs licked his blood at the pool of Samaria (22:37-38). Because of the postponement of the judgment, the dogs licked his son Joram's blood on Naboth's property, just as Elijah predicted (2 Kings 9:14-37). Later events proved that Ahab's repentance was short-lived, but the Lord at least gave him another opportunity to turn from sin and obey the Word. How much more evidence did Ahab need? But the influence of his wife couldn't easily be broken, for when Ahab married her, he sold himself into sin.

5. Receiving God's judgment (1 Kings 22:1-53; 2 Chron. 18)

At this point we are introduced to godly Jehoshaphat, king of Judah. A summary of his reign is found in 22:41-50 and even more fully in 2 Chronicles 17–20. He followed in the way of David and sought to please the Lord (17:1-6). He sent teaching priests throughout the land to explain God's law to the people (17:7-9) and assigned the other priests to serve as faithful judges to whom the people could bring their disputes. God gave Judah peace and Jehoshaphat took advantage of this opportunity to fortify the land (17:10-19).

He was a good king and a godly leader, but he got involved in three costly compromises. The first was the "bride compromise" when he married his son to a daughter of Ahab and Jezebel (2 Chron. 18:1; 21:4-7; 1 Kings 22:44; 2 Kings 8:16-19). This led to the "battle compromise," when Jehoshaphat got entangled in affairs of his son's father-in-law when Syria attacked Israel (18:2–19:3). Ahab's evil influence affected the reign of Jehoshaphat's grandson Ahaziah (2 Chron. 22:1-9), and the "battle compromise" almost cost Jehoshaphat his life (1 Kings 22:32-33). The third compromise was the "boat compromise," when Jehoshaphat foolishly joined forces with Ahab's son Ahaziah (1 Kings 22:48-49; 2 Chron. 20:31-37) and tried to get rich by importing foreign goods. The Lord wrecked his fleet and rebuked him for his sinful alliance.

One of Jehoshaphat's great achievements was the defeat of the Moabites, Ammonites, and Edomites, a great force that attacked Judah (2 Chron. 20:10). The king humbled himself before the Lord, called for a nationwide fast and encouraged the people to seek the face of the Lord. At a mass meeting in Jerusalem, Jehoshaphat prayed for God's guidance and help, reminding the Lord of His covenant with Abraham (v. 7), and God's acceptance of Solomon's prayer when he dedicated the temple (vv. 8-

9; 6:12–7:22). If the people would look toward the temple and prayed, God promised He would hear and answer. The Lord could see the great army approaching and the king asked Him to judge them. (The name "Jehoshaphat" means "whom God judges," that is, "God pleads his cause.")

The prayer was followed by a declaration of the Word from Jehaziel (20:14-17), assuring the king and his people that the Lord would indeed intervene and give Judah victory. "The battle is not yours, but God's" (v. 15). The king and the people believed the Lord's promise and praised Him even before the battle started. The next day, Jehoshaphat sent the army out with the singers at the very front! God caused the three enemy armies to fight among themselves and destroy themselves, leaving the spoils of war for the army of Judah. The army had praised God before the battle and at the very time of the battle, and now they praised him at the temple after the battle. Faith, prayer, and praise are great weapons!

In chapter 22, the writer of 1 Kings focused primarily on the "battle compromise."

Ahab compromises God's king (vv. 1-6). When after three years, Ben-hadad hadn't kept his agreement to give Israel back the cities his father took (21:34), Ahab decided it was time to fight Syria and take them back. Jehoshaphat's son was married to Ahab's daughter, so Jehoshaphat had to be friendly toward Ahab and help him fight his battles. He was disobeying the Lord when he took this step (2 Chron. 19:1-3), but one compromise often leads to another. As the descendant of David, Jehoshaphat should have kept his distance from Ahab and never allowed the Davidic line to mingle with that of Ahab. All the court chaplains,[6] paid to agree with the king, assured Ahab that he would win the battle, but Jehoshaphat was wise enough to ask Ahab for some Word from the Lord.

Yes, there was a prophet of the Lord in Israel, and he was where true prophets are often found—in prison. Ahab sent for his enemy Micaiah, and while the two kings were waiting, the prophets put on quite a demonstration. Zedekiah, who seemed to be their leader, made some iron horns to illustrate how Israel would push back and gore the Syrians and win the battle. All the other prophets agreed and shouted their approval. But it takes more than enthusiasm to win a war, especially when God has decreed otherwise.

Ahab ignores God's warning (vv. 7-28). Micaiah was under a great deal of pressure to agree with the false prophets and assure Ahab he would defeat Syria. Not only was Micaiah outnumbered four hundred to one, but the officer who brought him to the two kings warned him to agree with the majority. Often in Scripture, it's the *minority* that's in the will of God, and Micaiah was determined to be faithful, not popular. The sight of the two kings on their thrones, dressed in their royal robes, must have been impressive, but it didn't sway Micaiah. His words in verse 13 were spoken in sarcasm and Ahab knew it, but Ahab's reply wasn't honest. He was just trying to impress Jehoshaphat and make him think he really did want to know and do God's will.

The Lord had given Micaiah two visions, both of which announced judgment to King Ahab. In the first, he saw Israel wandering hopelessly, like sheep without a shepherd, obviously a description of a nation without a leader (Num. 27:15-22). Jesus used this image to depict the Jewish people without spiritual direction (Matt. 9:36). Ahab got the message: he would be killed in the battle.

The second vision explained how this would be accomplished: a lying spirit would give Ahab false confidence so he would enter the battle. That the God of truth should allow a lying spirit to accomplish His work is a puzzle to some people, but it's no different from God permitting Satan to attack Job (Job 1–2) or to motivate Judas to betray Jesus (John 13:21-30). God deals with people on the basis of their character. "With the pure You will show Yourself pure; and with the devious [crooked, NIV] You will show Yourself shrewd" (Ps. 18:26, NKJV). Ahab was fighting against God, and like any good boxer or wrestler, the Lord anticipated his moves and countered with the right response. Ahab was a consummate liar and the Lord dealt with him according to his character.

God didn't lie to Ahab; quite the contrary, through the lips of Micaiah He told the truth and gave Ahab fair warning of what lay ahead. The fact that God warned Ahab *before the battle* clears the Lord of the charge of being guilty of his death. The reaction of Zedekiah proves that the four hundred false prophets didn't believe Micaiah either. A much greater mystery is why a godly man like King Jehoshaphat went into the battle at all and risked his life. Ahab ordered the true prophet to be taken back to prison and given bread and water, as if punishing the prophet would change his message. The test of a true prophet was the actual fulfillment of his words (Deut. 18:17-22; Num. 16:29), and Micaiah knew this. That's why his parting message to Ahab was, "If you ever return in peace, the Lord has not spoken by me" (v. 28, NKJV).

Ahab meets his death (vv. 29-40, 51-53). How could King Jehoshaphat not discern what Ahab was doing to him? If Ahab had put a target on Jehoshaphat's back, he would not have made it easier for the enemy to kill him! If Jehoshaphat had died, then his son would have taken the throne, and Ahab's daughter would have been the Jezebel of Judah! If Ahab then united the two thrones and blended the Davidic line with his own line, what would have happened to the Davidic covenant and the Messianic line? But God is sovereign in all things and protected Jehoshaphat, while at the same time allowing a random arrow to hit an opening in Ahab's armor and kill him. Ahab was disguised and yet was killed, while Jehoshaphat was in his royal robes and never touched. Ahab had set the king of Syria free when he should have destroyed him, and now the Syrians killed Ahab.

Micaiah's prophecy was fulfilled and so were the prophecies of Elijah (20:42; 21:19-21).

Ahab's son Ahaziah took the throne and continued the evil ways of his father and mother (vv. 51-53). He reigned only two years, and his brother Joram (or Jehoram) succeeded him. The prophecy about the dogs licking blood on Naboth's property was actually fulfilled in the death of Joram (21:29; 2 Kings 9:25-26).

THIRTEEN

Reflections on Responsibility

Newspaper columnist Abigail Van Buren wrote, "If you want your children to keep their feet on the ground, put some responsibility on their shoulders." Responsibility isn't a curse; it's a blessing. Adam and Eve had work to do in paradise before sin came into the world, and the perfect Son of God worked as a carpenter before He began His public ministry. Booker T. Washington said, "Few things help an individual more than to place responsibility upon him, and to let him know that you trust him."

After killing his brother Abel and lying about it, Cain asked, "Am I my brother's keeper?" He was dodging both responsibility and accountability, a practice that's becoming very popular today. A bumper sticker announces, "The Devil made me do it" and people smile when they read it. When our first parents sinned, they ran and hid from God, and when they were confronted with their sin, they blamed others. Finally, they had to take the responsibility for what they had done, and with responsibility came hope and promise. Irresponsible people may run away, make excuses, cover up, or blame others, but if they do, they will never know the meaning of healthy character, integrity, a clear conscience, and the joy of walking with God.

First Kings begins with the death of King David and ends with the death of King Ahab, and between those two events many other people either succeeded or failed, lived or died, because of decisions that were either responsible or irresponsible. The world of David and Ahab was nothing like our world today, but human nature hasn't changed and the basic principles of life are quite stable. We ought to be able to reflect on what we've learned from 1 Kings and draw some practical conclusions for life today.

1. David: One person can make a difference

The more you ponder the life of David, warts and all, the more you see his greatness. He was born with leadership ability, courage, and practical common sense, and the Holy Spirit gave him sensitivity to God's will and a special power that set him apart as God's man. His predecessor King Saul almost destroyed the nation, but David accepted the difficult responsibility of putting it back together again and building it into a mighty kingdom. David defeated Israel's enemies; collected great treasures for building the temple; organized the army, the government, and the ministry at the sanctuary; wrote songs for the Levites to sing; and even invented musical instruments for them to play. What a man!

God's covenant with David assured Israel of a king forever and was ultimately fulfilled in the coming of Jesus Christ into the world. It was because of His promise to David that the Lord kept one of his descendants on the throne during the years of Judah's decline. Throughout the history of the monarchy, God measured every king against David, and though some of them were exceptional, none of them quite reached his level.

One person can make a difference, if that person is willing to accept responsibility and walk with God. Anybody can run with the herd, but when God finds individuals who are willing to stand alone if necessary, He goes to work and builds leaders. The words of Dr. Lee Roberson have echoed in my mind for many years: "Everything rises or falls with leadership."

2. Solomon: Success often leads to failure

It's good to have the things that money can buy, provided you
don't lose the things that money can't buy. Solomon was a bril-
liant man who could discuss everything from how to grow herbs
to how to build fortresses, yet he made a mess out of his life and
paved the way for the division of the kingdom. During the gold-
en age of Solomon, the nations marveled at his wisdom and
envied his wealth (and perhaps his many wives), but Solomon
himself turned out to be a hollow man who forsook the Lord who
had so richly blessed him. He was perhaps the wisest fool in Bible
history.

When you read between the lines, you find that his living in
luxury, surrounded by glamour and pleasure, introduced into
Israel the viruses that eventually ate the spiritual heart out of the
nation. Yes, we need education, but we also need to ask God for
the wisdom to use it as we should. We also need money for food,
clothing, and shelter—"For your heavenly Father knows that you
need all these things," said Jesus (Matt. 6:32)—but to acquire
money just for money's sake is to surrender to covetousness and
become so concerned about prices that we ignore values.

Solomon was irresponsible in many areas of life, and his son
Rehoboam inherited some of that mind-set and ended up dividing the nation. God made a leader out of David by sending him
out to care for sheep; challenging him with a lion, a bear, and a
giant; forcing him to run for his life for ten years; and making
him wait for the promised throne. Solomon grew up pampered
and protected; he could have used a few years' service in the
wilderness. By accumulating wives, horses, and wealth, he
brought peace to the nation, but it was a peace purchased at the
price of obedience to the law of God.

There's no virtue in ignorance and poverty, but there's no
magic in knowledge and wealth. The government leaders tell us,
"If people were just smarter and richer, we'd solve society's problems." People do become smarter and richer, and they create a
whole new set of problems. Billy Sunday once said, "When I was
a kid, we'd go down to the railroad yard and steal things from the

freight cars. Now a fellow goes to university and learns how to steal the whole railroad!" People are so smart they can sit at a computer keyboard and rob a bank thousands of miles away. Human nature doesn't change.

3. National strength and national character begin in the home

If David had displayed in his home the kind of discipline and strength he showed on the battlefield, Jewish history might have been different. Part of the problem lay with his having too many wives, plus the fact that it isn't always easy for the children of celebrities to grow up normally. But whatever the causes, some of David's children turned out really bad, and what they were and what they did affected the nation.

According to Genesis 3, Satan came as a liar and his first target was human marriage. He's been attacking it every since. According to Genesis 4, he came as a murderer and his second target was the human family. He encouraged Cain to be envious and angry so that Cain would kill Abel. It's been said that in the modern home, the stereo and the TV set are better adjusted than the members of the family. People complain because children can't pray in school, but few parents encourage them to pray at home.

Home is a school for character, where we learn to love, listen, obey, and assist. In short, it's where we learn to be responsible.

4. Rehoboam: Generations must work together

Whether it's in the home, in the chambers of government, or in the sanctuary of the local church, generations must work together and learn from each other. Solomon's son Rehoboam foolishly turned a deaf ear to the experience of the mature and chose to win only the applause of his peers, and as a result he lost most of his kingdom. By putting labels on different generations and letting them do their own thing—"Well, that's just the way they are!"—we've weakened social solidarity, divided the family, cut whole generations off from the heritage of the past, and convinced young people that they can really make it alone.

God has decreed that parents shall be older than their children. He has also commanded parents to love their children, teach them how to listen and obey, protect them from evil, and be good examples before them. But parents can also learn from their children. It's a two-way street. I cultivate the friendship of young people, because I need them and they need me. I help them catch up on the past and they help me catch up on the present. I'm not always right and they're not always wrong. The older generation hands the next generation a valuable heritage from the past, but if we don't understand the world they're living in and the way they feel about it, we can't help them use that heritage for their good and the good of society.

Paul saw the local church as a family in God (Titus 2:1-8), with one generation ministering to another. Younger people treat the older folks as they would their parents or grandparents, and older saints treat the younger ones as they would their own children. When a family gets together, they don't always agree on everything, but they try to help each other during the various stages of life. That's the way it should be in the home, the church, and the nation.

5. Jeroboam: wasted opportunity

God offered Jeroboam a priceless opportunity to build the kingdom of Israel for the glory of God, but he wasted it. Instead of looking back to David and imitating his leadership, and looking up to the Lord for help, Jeroboam let his ego take over and did things his own way. He invented his own religion to make it easy for the people to disobey the Lord. He abandoned the divine authority of God's Word and appointed priests who were unspiritual and unqualified. God sent him signs and messages, but he refused to submit. "The sins of Jeroboam" are mentioned over twenty times in Scripture.

The division of the Jewish nation was a tragedy, but if both Rehoboam and Jeroboam had listened to the Lord, they could have rescued both kingdoms from ruin. Once opportunity is lost, it won't be repeated. Each opportunity is a test of the vision and values of the people in charge. The Lord gave Jeroboam a sure promise (11:29-40), but the king wouldn't take it seriously and trust God to fulfill it. Opportunity doesn't shout, it whispers, and our ears must be attentive. Opportunity knocks, it doesn't kick down the door, and we had better be alert to open the door. The American poet John Greenleaf Whittier wrote

> For of all sad words of tongue or pen,
> The saddest are these: "It might have been!"

To ignore God-given opportunity is to waste the past, jeopardize the future, and frustrate the present.

6. Baal: The insidious cancer of idolatry

Jeroboam put up his golden calves and Jezebel brought in Baal worship, and before long, the people of the Northern Kingdom had turned from Jehovah to the worship of dumb idols. An idol is not only an insult to God but it's an insult to man, for men and women were created in the image of God to reflect the glory of the true and living God. To create a god in your own image and worship it is a dangerous thing, for we become like the gods we worship (Ps. 115:8).

If you want to be religious and still enjoy the pleasures of sin, then the worship of idols is the road to take. But its freedom leads to bondage and its pleasures eventually lead to pain and death. Whether the idol we worship is money, prestige, authority, sex, entertainment, or our own self-righteous satisfaction, it can never equal what we receive when we worship the true and living God through His Son Jesus Christ.

7. Elijah: Reformation and renewal

A nation, a church, a family, or an individual is never so far-gone that the Lord can't gave a new beginning. Elijah was Ahab's enemy because Ahab was following his own agenda and not the Lord's. Elijah was God's servant and risked his life to bring the nation back to the God of Abraham, Isaac, and Jacob. True reformation should lead to spiritual renewal. It isn't enough to tear down the pagan altars and remove the priests of Baal. We must rebuild the Lord's altar and ask God for new fire from heaven to consume the sacrifices.

Reformation means getting rid of the accretions of the new things to get back to the foundations of the old things. When Israel abandoned her covenant with Jehovah, she ceased to be the people of God and became like the other nations. The beautiful temple that once housed the glory of God became a pile of ruins that bore witness to the sins of an ungrateful and unbelieving people. God's chosen people forgot their glorious past and deliberately manufactured a future that brought shame and ruin.

The key issue in any nation's faith has always been the struggle between the true prophets and the false prophets, both of whom claim to speak in the name of the Lord. The false prophets tell us what we want to hear while the true prophets tell us what we need to hear. The false prophets don't make a deep and thorough diagnosis of the nation's sicknesses; they barely scratch the surface. True prophets cut deep and expose the hidden cancers; like John the Baptist, they apply the ax to the root of the trees (Matt. 3:10) and don't waste their time plucking off dead leaves from the dying branches.

"Where is the Lord God of Elijah?" asked Elisha as he began his prophetic ministry (2 Kings 2:14, NKJV). We know the answer: "The Lord is in his holy temple" (Hab. 2:20). But the real question isn't "Where is the Lord God of Elijah?" but "Where are the Elijahs?" God is still seeking for men and women whose hearts are right with Him, people He can use to recover the past, renew the present, and rescue the future.

8. Ahab and Jezebel: the abuse of power

Some years ago I began to read a biography of Adolph Hitler, but the longer I read it, the more depressed I became, until finally I stopped reading the book. I never did finish it. I respond the same way to Ahab and Jezebel. He was spineless and she was heartless and together they were the embodiment of wickedness.

If they were living today, Hollywood would make a feature movie about them and they'd be featured in a miniseries on television. Cameras in hand, the press would follow their every move and report every activity in detail. It would make no difference that Ahab and Jezebel were godless unbelievers who lacked character and high ideals. The public feeds its sick imagination on that kind of garbage and keeps asking for more. Thanks to fallen human nature, there's always more.

Page through a review of the twentieth century and marvel at how the nations of the world ever survived such a concerted abuse of power. Much of it was brutal, leading to the annihilation of millions of innocent people. Some of it was done with finesse, the abusers wearing their white gloves, but it still led to destruction. Abusers who didn't use knives, guns, and ovens, used words, and this includes professed Christians in the church. The world looked on and said, "Behold, how they hate one another!" I've been in ministry for over fifty years, and in the past ten years, I've heard more church horror stories than I did in the previous forty years.

Whether it's administrative power, financial power, physical and mental power, or the ultimate power of life and death, the power we have comes from God and must be used according to His will. King and queens, emperors and prime ministers, dictators and generals, parents and teachers, the FBI and the KGB—all of them are accountable to the Lord and will one day answer to Him.

King Jesus is the greatest example of the right use of authority. He is a Servant who leads and a Leader who serves, and He does it because He loves us.

9. God is sovereign!

Since the days of Job, people have been trying to make sense out of what goes on in this world, and nobody has yet discovered the key. We have a hard enough time predicting the weather let alone fully understanding the dynamics of history or even the personal situations in our own lives. A famous movie star said,

"Life is like a B-picture script. It is that corny. If I had my life story offered to me to film, I'd turn it down."[1] American playwright Eugene O'Neill had a character in *Strange Interlude* say, "Our lives are merely strange dark interludes in the electric display of God the Father." That's not very encouraging.

Knowing that our God is sovereign in all things gives us the courage and faith we need to live and serve in this fallen world. "The Lord brings the counsel of the nations to nothing; He makes the plans of the peoples of no effect. The counsel of the Lord stands forever, the plans of His heart to all generations" (Ps. 33:10-11, NKJV). He has given us the right to make choices and decisions, and He will not force His will upon us; but if He isn't allowed to rule, He will overrule. In spite of our resistance and rebellion, His will shall be done "on earth as it is in heaven." He runs the universe by His wise decrees and doesn't call a committee meeting to find the consensus of His creatures. "Man's will is free," writes A. W. Tozer, "because God is sovereign. A God less than sovereign could not bestow moral freedom upon His creatures. He would be afraid to do so."[2]

Yet, how longsuffering God is with both the saved and the lost! He allowed Jezebel to kill some of the prophets of the Lord, and He allowed Elijah to run away from the place of duty. The greatest judgment God can send is to allow people to have their own way and then suffer the consequences. "How long, O Lord, how long?" has been the painful prayer of believers on earth (Ps. 13:1-2) and in heaven (Rev. 6:10), but our times are in His hands and He knows the end from the beginning. When the news of the day upsets me, I pause and worship the eternal sovereign God who is never surprised or caught unprepared. This keeps me from fretting and getting discouraged and it helps to keep my life in balance.

The Book of 1 Kings has revealed to us the sinfulness of the human heart, the faithfulness of a loving God, and the seriousness of being a part of God's believing remnant. Before Jesus returns to set up His kingdom, many things are going to get worse and we may become discouraged and be tempted to quit. Then we'll remember that responsibility means our response to His ability. God is still on the throne, so we'll join the heavenly multitude and sing the song of the overcomers: "Alleluia, for the Lord God omnipotent reigneth" (Rev. 19:6, KJV).

NOTES

Chapter One

1. We aren't able to identify with certainty Shimei and Rei (v. 8), unless they were David's brothers Shimea and Raddai who held offices in the kingdom (1 Chron. 2:13-14, NIV). There was also a Shimei, son of Ela, who served in Solomon's court (1 Kings 4:18). The Shimei in 1 Kings 1:8 certainly wasn't the same Shimei who cursed David during Absalom's rebellion (2 Sam. 16:5-12; 19:18-23).

2. David ruled over a united kingdom, so the phrase "over Israel and over Judah" seems strange to us. But this record was written many years after these events occurred and after the kingdom had been divided.

3. 1 Chronicles 29:23-25 records another coronation service for Solomon. Whether this is the same one described in 1 Kings 1 or a later celebration that was larger and more carefully planned, we can't be sure. It seems unlikely that the ailing David got up from his deathbed, made the speeches recorded in 1 Chronicles 28:1–29:20, witnessed Solomon's second anointing, and then returned to his room to die. 1 Chronicles 29:22 states that Solomon was "acknowledged as king" and anointed "a second time," so the event in 1 Kings 1 has to be his first. It possible that the author of Chronicles dropped this information in at this point as a summary of the last events in the life of David (29:21-30). In times of crisis, it wasn't unusual for the new king to have a hasty coronation and then a larger and more formal one later. There are some chronological problems here, but in view of the volatile situation, it isn't impossible that God gave David strength to participate in the great public events described in 1 Chronicles 28–29. Solomon's second anointing was necessary to establish once and for all that he was indeed the king. David was anointed three times (1 Sam. 16:13; 2 Sam. 2:4 and 5:3).

4. Since Adonijah was the leader of the rebellion, he was the most responsible. Solomon not only pardoned Adonijah but he also pardoned the other sons of David who were at the feast (1:9). Solomon realized that they had been duped by Adonijah and attended the feast in innocence. One there, they discovered the reason for the celebration, but it would

have been dangerous to leave, knowing that all the army officers were there. Jonathan's news report gave them the opportunity they needed to escape.

5. Chronologists don't find it easy to calculate Solomon's age at his accession to the throne, nor do we know how long David lived after Solomon became coregent. David was thirty years old when he began to reign in Hebron (2 Sam. 5:1-5), and he reigned seven years there and thirty-three years in Jerusalem, making him seventy years old when he died. If he was fifty when he committed adultery with Bathsheba, and if Solomon was the son born next after the death of their baby (2 Sam. 12:24-25), then Solomon could have been eighteen or nineteen years old when he became king. However, 1 Chronicles 3:5 suggests strongly that Solomon was their fourth son, which could make him as young as fifteen when he became king. David described Solomon as "young and tender [inexperienced, NIV]" (1 Chron. 22:5, KJV), but perhaps this was the language of an aged father as he looked at his successor. Raised in the security of the palace, Solomon wasn't the well-rounded man that his father was; but does any leader think his son is ready to take over?

6. For examples of kings obeying God's law, see 2 Kings 14:6; 18:4, 6.

Chapter Two

1. Frederick Buechner, *Peculiar Treasures* (New York: Harper and Row, 1979), p. 161.

2. Solomon's wife's dowry from Pharaoh was the Philistine city of Gezer (1 Kings 9:16). Egypt had conquered Philistia and still held authority over it. This was not Solomon's first wife, because his first-born son and successor, Rehoboam, had an Ammonite mother named Naamah (14:21). Solomon must have married before he became king because Rehoboam was forty-one years old when he took the throne, and Solomon reigned forty years.

3. The Jews were not to marry the women who belonged to the pagan nations in the land of Canaan (Ex. 34:16; Deut. 7:1ff), a law that Solomon eventually violated. There seemed to be no regulation concerning a Jew taking an Egyptian wife. Jewish tradition says that his wife did adopt the Jewish faith.

4. They were called "high places" (*bamah*) because they were usually located in the hills, away from the cities, in the midst of nature and "closer" to heaven. The word *bamah* means "elevation." Worship at these pagan shrines usually involved unspeakable orgies. Some Jews worshiped Baal at the high places during the period of the Judges (Jud. 6:25; 13:16). During the days of Samuel and Saul, sacrifices weren't always offered at the tabernacle altar (1 Sam. 7:10; 9:11-25; 13:9; 14:35; 16:5). David built an altar on Mount Moriah (1 Chron. 21:26), no doubt anticipating the day when the temple would stand there. Worship at the high places was a constant temptation and sin during the days of the Jewish monarchy, and no sooner did one king destroy these pagan shrines than his successor would rebuild them.

5. See my book on Proverbs, *Be Skillful* (Victor, 1995).

6. Two different Hebrew words are translated "understanding" in this passage. In verse 9, the word *shama* means "to hear, listen, obey." The Hebrew daily confession of faith is called "the Shema," and begins "Hear, O Israel . . . " (Deut. 6:4-5). The word used in verses 11-12 is *bin* and means "to distinguish, to discern, to separate." Together, the words mean "to hear with the intention to obey, and to exercise discernment so as to understand."

7. The Bible records four times when God spoke to Solomon: at Gibeon (3:10-15), during the building of the temple (6:11-13), after the completion of his building projects (9:3-9), and when Solomon disobeyed the Lord and worshiped idols (11:9-13). Note that in the first three instances, the emphasis was on obedience.

8. Solomon didn't need 40,000 horses when he had only 1,400 chariots (1 Kings 10:26; 2 Chron. 1:14), so the figure 4,000 in 2 Chronicles 9:25 is no doubt the correct one. If each chariot had two horses, that would leave 1,200 horses for the fortress cities Solomon had armed and also for other state services.

9. *Bible Characters from the Old and New Testaments* (Kregel: 1990), p. 284.

Chapter Three

1. After the Babylonian captivity, the Jewish remnant began to rebuild the temple at the same time of the year (Ezra 3:8).

2. 2 Chronicles 2:14 identifies his mother with Dan, not Naphtali, but when you remember how Solomon established new districts and borders, this is no problem. The tribes of Dan and Naphtali were united in the eighth district of Naphtali, supervised by Ahimaaz (4:15).

3. Hiram also provided Solomon with wood for his palace complex. Apparently Solomon ran up a bill he couldn't pay immediately because Hiram also loaned him some gold. As collateral, Solomon gave Hiram twenty cities on the border of Galilee and Phoenicia, but Hiram wasn't pleased with them (1 Kings 9:10-14). Later, Solomon was able to pay his debt and reclaim the cities (2 Chron. 8:1). Of course, all these payments of food and gold came out of the pockets of the Jewish people, so it's no wonder they protested and asked for relief after Solomon died (1 Kings 12:1-15).

4. The height of the temple was forty-five feet, which meant there was an "attic space" fifteen feet high above the Holy of Holies. We aren't told if or how this space was used.

5. 2 Chronicles 3:15 gives the height of the pillars as thirty-five cubits, which some take to mean the *combined* height.

6. 1 Kings 7:26 says the basin held 2,000 baths, or about 11,000 gallons of water, while 2 Chronicles 4:5 says 3,000 baths or over 17,000 gallons. The larger amount may have been its full capacity while the smaller amount was what was normally kept in the molten sea. Water was a precious commodity in the east and it would take a lot of labor to fill up the huge basin.

Chapter Four

1. The sequence of events as recorded in 1 Kings appears to be as follows. First, the temple structure was built in seven years (6:1-38). Then, the royal palaces were built in thirteen years (7:1-12), making a total of twenty years for all this construction (9:10). During that time, Hiram was constructing the furnishings of the temple and supervising the work within the building (7:13-51). When all this work was completed, Solomon dedicated the temple (8:1-66), following which God appeared to Solomon the second time (9:1-9). The Lord's words to Solomon in 9:3 [2 Chron. 7:12] are not as meaningful if the dedication had taken place thirteen years before.

2. The text mentions the city of David (v. 1), God's choice of David (v. 16), and especially God's covenant with David (vv. 15-18, 20, 24-26). The Lord kept His promise and gave David a son who built the temple that David wanted to build (v. 20). When the people left the dedication service and the feast that followed, they rejoiced at the good things the Lord had "done for David" (v. 66).

3. David's first attempt to bring the ark to Jerusalem failed miserably, but his second attempt was successful. Solomon followed his father's example by offering many sacrifices as the priests carried the ark from the city of David to the temple. However, unlike his father, Solomon didn't dance in the holy procession.

4. Amos 4 describes how God did send many of these judgments to the kingdom of Israel.

5. It's generally accepted by students that Psalm 132 was composed for use when the ark was brought to the temple and the temple was dedicated. The petitioner asked God to bless the king (Solomon) for the sake of David (vv. 1, 10), that is, because of the covenant God made with David in 2 Samuel 7. David wanted to build the temple (vv. 2-9), but God chose his son to do it. The Lord also promised to keep David's descendants on the throne (vv. 11-12, 17) and defeat Israel's enemies (v. 18).

Chapter Five

1. The timber and the stones had to be brought from a distance and the stones carefully cut to fit into the structure without any further dressing. All of this took time. Doing the delicate gold work within the temple, plus making the many pieces of furniture and utensils, would also require time. This explains why it took twenty years to finish both structures.

2. Nothing is said about Solomon's wife Naamah, the Ammonitess, who gave birth to Rehoboam, Solomon's firstborn son and successor (14:21).

3. Control of the cities would give Hiram whatever resources were available, including taxing the citizens or conscripting them for service. It was not a nice way for Solomon to treat his own people.

4. "The Deserted Village" by Oliver Goldsmith, lines 51 and 52.

5. It's futile to connect the number 666 with Revelation 13:18. When you add Hiram's loan of 120 talents of gold (9:14) with the 420 talents brought in by the navy (9:28) and the 120 talents given by the queen of Sheba (10:10), you have a total of 660 talents of gold. It is said that the number six in Scripture is the number of man, always short of the number seven, the perfect number that belongs only to God. If this is true, then Solomon's 666 talents represents man's ultimate wealth, not the true eternal wealth that comes only from God. We brought nothing into this world, and we shall take nothing out (1 Tim. 6:7; Job 1:21; Ps. 49:17).

Chapter Six

1. *Expositions of Holy Scripture*, by Alexander Maclaren, on 1 Kings 11:4-13.

2. I like F. W. Robertson's definition of "the world." You find it in volume 4 of his collected sermons, p. 165. "The world is that collection of men in every age who live only according to the maxims of their time." In amassing wealth and multiplying wives, and in his desire to live in splendor, Solomon was imitating the eastern potentates and not following the Word of God or the example of his father David.

3. In spite of what songwriters say, crossing the Jordan and entering the land of Canaan is not a picture of going to heaven. We certainly won't have to fight our way into heaven! It's a picture of turning our back on the past and entering by faith into our present inheritance in Christ, the blessings He wants us to enjoy, and the work He wants us to do. All of this is explained in the Book of Hebrews.

4. For instances of prophets courageously confronting kings, see 13:1-10; 14:1-18; 16:1-4; 20:22ff; 22:1ff; 2 Kings 1.

5. Samuel had ripped Saul's garment and used the event to preach a message (1 Sam. 15:27), and David had cut a piece from Saul's garment (1 Sam. 24:4-6). The image is an obvious one.

6. Students of Old Testament history have noted that early in the nation's history, there was rivalry between the ten northern tribes and the two southern tribes, so it wasn't easy to divide the nation. See Judges 5:14-16; 2 Samuel 19:41-43; 20:2; 1 Kings 1:35; 4:20, 25. This rivalry will be healed when Messiah reigns (Isa. 11:13).

7. William Sanford LaSor, *Great Personalities of the Old Testament* (Revell, 1959), p. 125.

Chapter Seven

1. Some question that a man forty-one years old could be called "young and indecisive" (2 Chron. 13:7), but age and maturity are two different things. During the latter part of Solomon's reign, Rehoboam took eighteen wives and sixty concubines, and his family consisted of twenty-eight sons and sixty daughters (2 Chron. 11:18-21).

2. With two exceptions, when information is given about a king of Judah, the name of his mother is included. It was important that David's line be identified accurately. The exceptions are Jehoram (2 Kings 8:17) and Ahaz (2 Kings 16:2).

3. Some students think that Jeroboam was holding a meeting for the Northern Kingdom and Rehoboam saw this as an opportunity to get a hearing and build some bridges into the Northern Kingdom. If so, Rehoboam certainly turned a good opportunity into a terrible calamity.

4. The phrase "all Israel" can mean both kingdoms (9:30; 12:1) or only the northern ten tribes (10:16; 11:13). The reader must consider the context and be discerning.

5. Did this man have several names or were there three different men with similar names, each of whom served a different king? Adoram was over the forced labor when David was king (2 Sam. 20:24) and Adoniram when Solomon reigned (4:6). The man Rehoboam sent was named both Adoram and Hadoram (2 Chron. 10:18). It's difficult to believe that one man could serve so many years, but perhaps he did. Some students believe that three men are involved: Adoram served David, Adoniram served Solomon, and the first Adoram's son or grandson (Adoram/Hadoram) served Rehoboam. But would Rehoboam send an untried and relatively unknown officer on such an important diplomatic mission? It's more likely that Adoram is another form of Adoniram, the man who served Solomon, because it was Solomon's yoke that the people were opposing, not David's.

6. In David's last census, Joab reported 500,000 able-bodied men in Judah available to bear arms (2 Sam. 24:9), while there were 800,000 men available in the northern tribes. Those numbers were over forty

years old, but perhaps the population hadn't changed that much.

7. In 1 Kings 12:22, Shemiah is called "a man of God," a title often used for prophets, especially in 1 and 2 Kings (1 Kings 12:22; 13:1, 26; 17:18, 24; 20:28; 2 Kings 1:9, 11; 4:7, 9, 16, 22, 25, 27, 40, 42; 5:14). Moses bore this title (Deut. 33:1; Josh. 14:6) and Paul applied it to Timothy in 1Timothy 6:11, and to all dedicated believers in 3:17.

8. The Jewish people should be recognized and applauded for being the only nation in history that has left an accurate portrait of their leaders and a factual report of their history. The Bible is a Jewish book, yet it doesn't always show Israel in a good light. Of course, the Scriptures are inspired by God, but it still took a good deal of honesty and humility to write the record and admit that it is true.

9. In both Kings and Chronicles, the message of obedience and blessing comes through loud and clear. However, we must not conclude that everybody who obeys God will escape suffering and trial, for more than one good king had personal troubles, and some were assassinated. No king was perfect, but God's covenant with Israel assured them that He would bless the nation if they obeyed His will.

10. Abijah was also known as Abijam (1 Kings 14:31; 15:1, 7-8, KJV). This change in spelling may reflect a desire to eliminate from the name of an ungodly man (1 Kings 15:3) the syllable "Jah," which refers to Jehovah.

11.This theme is expanded and illustrated in the Book of Hosea. The Prophet Hosea's wife became a prostitute and he had to buy her back out of the slave market.

12. This is not the Pharaoh who made a treaty with Solomon and gave him a daughter to be his wife. The new Pharaoh was not friendly toward Judah.

Chapter Eight

1. Don't confuse Jeroboam I with Jeroboam II, Israel's fourteenth king, who reigned from 782–753. His history is found in 2 Kings 14:23-29.

2. It's unlikely that Aaron was trying to introduce a new god to Israel but rather was presenting Jehovah in the form of the golden calf (Ex. 32). The calf was supposed to be a "help" to the Jews in their worship

of the Lord. Aaron certainly knew that Jehovah was the only true God, but he also knew that the weak people couldn't live by faith in an invisible Jehovah, especially when their leader Moses had been absent for forty days. This fact doesn't exonerate Aaron, but it does help us better understand the mind-set of the people. It was easier to worship the invisible Lord by means of the visible calf, and it wasn't long before the idolatry gave birth to indecency and immorality (Ex. 32:6, 19; 1 Cor. 10:1-8). No matter what excuse Aaron gave, he had sinned in giving the people what they wanted and not what they needed. Jeroboam also gave the people what they wanted, and false teachers are doing the same thing today (2 Peter 2; Jude 1ff).

3. According to Exodus 29 Aaron and his sons needed for their consecration one bull for a sin offering, a ram for a burnt offering, and another ram for a fellowship offering. It took seven days for the consecration service to be completed. Obviously, Jeroboam wasn't following God's directions.

4. People talk about "the ten lost tribes of Israel," but this is not a biblical concept. God knows where children of Abraham are and He will call them together when it's time. Some nations have claimed to be the descendants of the so-called ten lost tribes, but these claims are unfounded. Jesus spoke of the "twelve tribes of Israel" (Matt. 19:28; Luke 22:30), and Paul spoke of "our twelve tribes" as living entities in his day (Acts 26:7), and James wrote his epistle to "the twelve tribes scattered abroad" (James 1:1, KJV). In his vision of future events, John the apostle saw twelve tribes sealed by God (Rev. 7:4) and twelve gates named for the twelve tribes (21:12).

5. Nowhere in Scripture do we read of any servant of the Lord "retiring" and doing nothing for the Lord as he waited to die. Instead of relocating in Judah, or staying in Israel to oppose the false religion, the old man accepted the *status quo* and became comfortable. Moses and the other prophets served to the very end, and there's no evidence that the apostles abandoned their calling when they became old. Dr. William Culbertson, for many years dean and then president of Moody Bible Institute in Chicago, often ended his public prayers with, "And, Lord, help us to end well."

6. Saul disguised himself and both Samuel and the witch saw

through it (1 Sam. 28). Wicked King Ahab disguised himself in battle, hoping King Jehoshaphat would be killed, but a random arrow hit him just the same (1 Kings 22:30ff). Godly King Josiah foolishly interfered with Pharaoh Neco, disguised himself, and was killed in battle (2 Chron. 35:20-25). God can see through disguises.

7. The prophet Nathan took a similar approach in confronting King David (2 Sam. 12:7-8a).

8. Thomas Jefferson, *Notes on Virginia*, in *The Life and Selected Writings of Thomas Jefferson*, edited by Adrienne Koch and William Peden (N.Y.: Modern Library), p. 258.

Chapter Nine

1. This interpretation of Rehoboam's foolish decision is that of his son and not that of the Lord. It did not come from an inspired prophet. We would expect a son to defend his father.

2. Joshua's victory at Jericho seems to be the backdrop for this event. The Lord is called "captain" (v. 12; Josh. 5:13-15, KJV), the priests blew the trumpets, and the people shouted (Josh. 6:1-21). The victory was completely from the Lord.

3. The calling of assemblies is a significant thing in the history of the Jews, both before and after the division of the kingdom. (See 1 Chron. 13:2-5; 28:8; 29:1; 2 Chron. 5:6; 20:3ff; 30:1ff.)

4. The fact that submitting to the covenant was a matter of life or death (2 Chron. 15:13) doesn't imply that Judah had become brutal or that the sword brought about the revival. Those who refused to seek God and renew the covenant were declaring that they were practicing idolatry, and according to Deuteronomy 13:6-9, idolaters were not to be spared. The people who refused to submit knew what the covenant said, so in declaring their allegiance to a foreign god, they were taking their own lives in their hands.

5. There's a chronological problem here since Baasha ascended the throne during Asa's third year and reigned for twenty-four years (1 Kings 15:33). This means he died in Asa's twenty-seventh or twenty-eighth year and therefore could not have attacked Judah in Asa's thirty-sixth year. Dr. Gleason Archer suggests that the word translated

"reign" in 2 Chronicles 16:1 (KJV, NIV) should be understood as "kingdom," that is, "in the thirty-sixth year of the kingdom of Judah." Therefore, the writer was dating this event from the division of the kingdom in 931–930, and not from Asa's accession to the throne in 910. The Hebrew word translated "reign" is translated "kingdom" or "realm" in 2 Chronicles 1:1, 11:17 and 20:30. Some students see these numbers as a copyist's error, for in the Hebrew, the difference between the letters used for 36 and 16 is very slight. See Archer's *Encyclopedia of Bible Difficulties* (Zondervan), pp. 225-226.

6. The inability of the physicians to help Asa must not be interpreted as a divine rejection of the medical profession. God can heal either with or without means (Isa. 38:21), and Paul had Luke "the beloved physician" on his missionary staff (Col. 4:14). Even Jesus said that sick people need a physician (Luke 5:27-32). To use 2 Chronicles 16:12 as an argument for "faith healing" and against going to the doctor is to misinterpret and apply a very plain statement. Asa's sickness was a judgment from the Lord, and his going to the physicians was a rebellion against the Lord. He refused to repent, so God refused to let him be healed.

7. Asa's body was placed in his prepared tomb. The burning had nothing to do with cremation, a practice that the Jews considered reprehensible.

8. The phrase "because he killed him" in verse 7 indicates that though Baasha fulfilled God's will when he killed Nadab and then wiped out the house of Jeroboam, he was still responsible for his motives and his actions. Baasha didn't enter into his grisly work as a holy servant of God but as an evil assassin who wanted the throne.

Chapter Ten

1. "Tishbite" probably refers to the town of Tishbe in Gilead, located west of Mahanaim.

2. The six-month period from April to October is the factor that explains the seeming discrepancy between 1 Kings 18:1 (three years) and Luke 4:25 and James 5:17 (three years and six months). When the expected early rains didn't appear in October, Elijah explained the cause. The drought was already six months old by the time Elijah visited Ahab.

3. On the schools of the prophets, see 1 Samuel 10:5 and 2 Kings 2:3-7 and 6:1-2.

4. The Hebrew word in verse 27 that is translated "pursuing" in the KJV and "busy" in the NIV can also mean "relieving himself." Idolaters make their gods in their own image.

5. Satan is a counterfeiter of the miracles of God (2 Thes. 2:9-10) and could have sent fire from heaven (Job 1:9-12; Rev. 13:13), but the Lord restrained him.

6. Some have suggested that Ahab ate some of the sacrificial meat, but that doesn't seem possible. Elijah's sacrifice was completely consumed and the sacrifice to Baal was never exposed to any fire.

Chapter Eleven

1. The Hebrew text reads "and when he saw," as do the KJV and the NIV margin. The Septuagint reads "he was afraid," and the NIV and the NASB both adopted this text. What did he see that made him afraid? The dangerous situation? The dangerous messenger? We aren't told and it's useless to speculate.

2. "Sitting under the juniper tree" is a common English phrase that describes a person who is angry at God, sick of life, embarrassed by failure, and ready to call it quits.

3. The scene reminds us of Jonah at Nineveh as he argued with the Lord (Jonah 4). Moses also wanted to die because of the impossible workload he tried to carry (Num. 11:14-15).

4. The Hebrew text of verse 9 reads "the cave" as if a well-known cave was meant. Some students believe that Elijah occupied the same part of Sinai that Moses did when he saw the glory of God (Ex. 33:12-23).

5. See Psalm 12:1, Micah 7:2, and Isa. 57:1.

6. *Robust in Faith* (Moody Press), p. 135.

7. Elijah called Elisha (19:19-21), and Elisha anointed Hazael (2 Kings 8:7-15). By the authority of his master, Elisha's servant anointed Jehu (2 Kings 9:1-10). From God's point of view, it was Elijah who did all of this.

8. Once again, we see the Lord calling people who were busy. This was true of Moses, Gideon, David, Nehemiah, Amos, and the apostles.

Chapter Twelve

1. As we have noted before, deciphering the transcription of numbers in the Hebrew language has sometimes caused problems for students, since letters are used for numbers and some letters look very similar. Could that many people be killed just by walls falling on them? But
the collapsing of the walls would leave the city defenseless and make it
possible for Ahab's troops to kill anybody seeking refuge in the city.
The seven days of waiting, the falling of the walls, and the deception
afterward all makes us think of the fall of Jericho (Josh. 6). However,
Ahab was certainly no Joshua!

2. God sometimes told the prophets to use "action sermons" to get
His message across to people who were spiritually blind and deaf. For
example, Isaiah dressed like a prisoner war for three years (Isa. 20);
Jeremiah wore a wooden yoke and then an iron one (Jer. 27–28); and
Ezekiel "played war," ate prisoners' rations, and cooked over a dung fire
(Ezek. 4).

3. Disguises seem to play a significant role in 1 Kings. See 14:2 and
22:30.

4. *The Knowledge of the Holy* (Harper, 1961), p. 11. See Psalm 50:21.

5. When in his refusal Naboth said "The Lord forbid" (v. 3), he was-
n't taking an oath or blaspheming God's name. But deceivers like
Ahab and Jezebel know how to turn nothing into something.
Exaggeration is a subtle form of lying.

6. The prophets of Baal had been slain (18:40) but could have been
replaced. However, knowing Jehoshaphat's devotion to the Lord, Ahab
wasn't likely to parade four hundred prophets of Baal before him. These
men were probably attached to the shrines at Dan and Bethel where
Jeroboam had put the golden calves. (See Amos 7:10-13.) It was still
idolatry, but of a more refined type. These false prophets used the name
of the Lord and claimed to speak by His authority (22:11-12). This is
the same kind of false prophet that Jeremiah had to put up with years
later.

Chapter Thirteen

1. Kirk Douglas in *Look*, Oct. 4, 1955.
2. *The Knowledge of the Holy* (Harper, 1961), p. 118.

Chapter One

Sunset and Sunrise
(1 Kings 1:1–2:46)

1. Who were the major players in the power struggle for succession to David's throne?

2. In what different ways do a real leader and an opportunist face a crisis? How can you develop the qualities of a leader?

3. Who was Abishag and how was she involved in the aftermath of David's death?

4. How did David's failures as a father contribute to the succession crisis? What can fathers today learn from this?

5. How was Bathsheba's influence seen in the palace at this time?

6. How did David make sure his choosing of Solomon was clear and known by all?

7. Why did Adonijah take hold of the horns of the altar?

8. How did David try to prevent his old conflicts from hindering Solomon's reign?

9. Why did Adonijah want to marry Abishag?

10. What changes should you make now so that at the end of your life you can, as David did, look back with satisfaction?

Chapter Two

Wisdom from Above
(1 Kings 3:1–4:34)

1. What contrasts does Wiersbe highlight between the lives of King David and his son Solomon?

2. How did Solomon build alliances with other nations? Why did this, as Wiersbe says, "cut at the very heart of Israel's unique position as people of God"?

3. What might "cut at the very heart of" contemporary believers' role as people of God?

4. What can we learn from how worldly beauty and the success of Israel was hiding inward decay?

5. Why was Gibeon a sacred place?

6. What were the Lord's command and question to Solomon? How did Solomon respond? How do you think you would have responded?

7. What is wisdom? How can we grow in wisdom? What is an "understanding heart"? How we can obtain this?

8. In order to live a long life full of blessing, what did Solomon need to do?

9. What does Wiersbe mean when he says, "the heart of every problem is a problem in the heart"?

10. What areas of life did Solomon's wisdom encompass? If he was so wise, how could he fall into sin?

Chapter Three

Fulfilling David's Dream
(1   K i n g s   5 : 1 – 6 : 3 8 ;   7 : 1 3 - 5 1)

1. How did David prepare the way for Solomon to build the temple?

2. What similarities are there between Moses' building of the tabernacle and Solomon's building of the temple?

3. Who were the "conscripted workers?" How did the Jewish people feel when Solomon conscripted the workers? When does this feeling show up in a significant way?

4. Who else helped to build the temple? Why is this fact significant?

5. In what way(s) is the church today God's temple?

6. What lesson can we learn from the way God used two of David's greatest sins? How does that encourage you?

7. If our work does not impress God (such as building the temple), then what does God truly want?

8. What was the water in the lavers for? What does this symbolize?

9. What is the point of everything, even the water basin stands, being elaborately beautiful?

10. What eventually happened to this incredible and costly temple? Why?

Chapter Four

God's House and Solomon's Heart
(1 Kings 8:1–9:9,25-28)

1. What made this temple more than just a building God commanded to be built, but the very "house of God"? Where, during our era, does God dwell?

2. In what ways was the presence of God's glory seen thus far in Israel's history?

3. How does the mystery of God (that which we don't always understand) affect us?

4. How is our dwelling in our home different than God dwelling in His house?

5. What seven specific requests did Solomon present to the Lord?

6. If we were to pray for justice in our land, how might we expect God to answer?

7. What were Solomon's reasons that God should forgive His people?

8. Why was it wise to include a review of God's faithfulness through Israel's history as Solomon blessed the people?

9. What was the sign that the Lord answered Solomon's request?

10. What did the peace offering symbolize?

Chapter Five

The Kingdom, Power, and Glory
(1 Kings 7:1-12; 9:10-10:29)

1. In the description of Solomon's palace, what character traits of Solomon's seem to surface?

2. In contrast to his father David being a mighty general, what were Solomon's strengths?

3. What did the celebrations of Passover, Harvest (or Weeks) and Ingathering (or Tabernacles or Booths) mean to the Jews?

4. What do Passover, Pentecost, and the Feast of Tabernacles mean to Christians?

5. What did the burnt, fellowship (peace), and incense offerings signify?

6. What was the purpose of the queen of Sheba's visit? What was her response?

7. As a man of unparalleled wealth, what does Solomon write in Ecclesiates about the value of wealth?

8. In referring to the queen of Sheba, what lesson did Jesus teach? (See Matt. 12:39-42.) How can you personally respond to that teaching?

9. As we study the incredible riches of Solomon, what do we learn about the possession of riches by a believer?

10. How can a person know if their riches are a sign of blessing from the Lord? What guidelines do you find for riches in 1 Timothy 6:17-19?

Chapter Six

The Foolish Wise Man
(1 Kings 11:1-43)

1. What were the four steps in Solomon's downward path?

2. Why did Solomon marry the Egyptian princess? Why did he marry the other foreign wives?

3. How did Solomon's marriages to foreign wives contribute to his descent to idolatry?

4. Why did Solomon buy so many horses and chariots? What would be the equivalent in our day? In what area of your life might you be trusting in "horses and chariots" instead of the Lord?

5. What do the wilderness and the Promised Land picture for the church today?

6. What warning did God give Solomon before and during his idolatry? What could Solomon have done at that point?

7. How did God keep His covenant with David even after Solomon's idolatry?

8. How did Solomon resist God's discipline? How would people know if it were God disciplining them? How should a believer respond to God's discipline?

9. Did Solomon ever return to the Lord? Give support for your answer.

10. What sin brought the downfall of the entire Jewish nation? In what way(s) is Solomon responsible for that?

Chapter Seven

He Would Not Listen
(1 Kings 12:1-24; 14:21-31)

1. What 4 characteristics of Rehoboam are highlighted?

2. How was King Solomon's relationship with the people different than that of King David?

3. Who was the leader of the northern ten tribes? How did he rise to leadership?

4. What did Jeroboam and the northern tribes request of Rehoboam? How did Rehoboam make his decision? What did he neglect to do? What was the result?

5. What approach to leadership is necessary for God's chosen leaders? How did Jesus exemplify this?

6. What does Wiersbe say is "the most important thing in spiritual leadership"? What does this mean?

7. Why is it important for all ages to fellowship together in their local church?

8. Why do you think it is often during the third generation that a ministry can be prone to fall apart?

9. During the first three years of the divided kingdom, how did the ten northern tribes and Judah perform with regard to keeping the law of Moses? To what do you attribute the difference between them? What happened in the fourth year?

10. When being disciplined by the Lord, how can Christians make a new beginning?

Chapter Eight

A New King, an Old Sin
(1 Kings 12:25-14:20)

1. What 3 serious mistakes did Jeroboam make as King?

2. According to Wiersbe, what does success in life depend upon? Do you agree? What might you add to that equation?

3. Why would fear be "one of the first evidences of unbelief"?

4. What human tendency did Jeroboam take advantage of as he started his new religion? When in your lifetime have you seen these tendencies in action?

5. What various commands of God did Jeroboam defy as he set up his religion?

6. How do we know Christianity is the only true religion?

7. What warnings came from God to Jeroboam? How did Jeroboam respond to these warnings?

8. What was the likely purpose of the miracles of the shriveling of Jeroboam's hand and the altar splitting?

9. Because the prophet was deceived and then he disobeyed, he was punished. What message should this have been to King Jeroboam? What warnings can believers today receive?

10. How did God speak to and through the blind prophet Ahijah? What explanation came through Ahijah as to the cause of the coming disasters?

Chapter Nine

Kings on Parade
(1 Kings 15:1-16:28)

1. With all the rebellion and idolatry of the Jewish nation, how is it possible that worship of the one true God and the coming of the Savior were accomplished through them?

2. Why were so few of Judah's kings proclaimed "good"?

3. When biblical chronologies of kings and their reigns seem to be inconsistent, and therefore cast doubt on the reliability of the Bible, how can this be explained?

4. Before the war between Judah and Israel, what message did Abijah, King of Judah, bring to Jeroboam and Israel? In the conflict that followed, how did the men of Judah achieve the victory? (See 2 Chron. 13:13-18.)

5. What was Asa like as a king? What did he accomplish?

6. Following in the steps of Asa, how could local church leaders today inspire a renewed commitment to the Lord?

7. What mistake did King Asa make when Israel was about to attack Judah? When have you made this same mistake?

8. How and why did Jeroboam's reign come to an end?

9. How can we tell Baasha did not learn from history? What did a prophet tell Baasha his destiny would be?

10. If a person's sin fulfills the prophetic unfolding of God's will, how can he or she be accountable before God? Why?

Chapter Ten

Let the Fire Fall
(1 Kings 17:1–18:46)

1. Where in the New Testament is Elijah mentioned?

2. What seven miracles did Elijah either perform or experience?

3. How far in advance did God reveal His unfolding plan for Elijah? What can we learn from this?

4. What other type of drought was there while Elijah stepped out of public ministry? When have you felt this drought in your life? What brought it to an end?

5. God's command to Elijah to go to the widow did not make sense, but Elijah went and was provided for. What lessons can we learn from this?

6. Elijah showed great faith in God as he pleaded for the boy to receive back his life. What does God reveal about Himself in this account?

7. When Jesus referred to the story of Elijah and the widow (Luke 4:16-20), what point was He making? How did the Jews respond?

8. How did God use Obadiah in his sphere of influence?

9. How did Elijah phrase his request to the Lord to come down in fire? What was Elijah's goal?

10. What can we learn about prayer from Elijah's request that God send the rain and from God's response?

Chapter Eleven

The Cave Man
(1 K i n g s 1 9 : 1 - 2 1)

1. What happened to Elijah after the great victory on Mount Carmel? How can we prepare for the trials that may follow our great victories?

2. What four messages was Elijah responding to in 1 Kings 19?

3. What other biblical characters also failed in their strongest point? What is your strongest point? How can you avoid failure in that area?

4. What did Elijah need to get back on track with the Lord?

5. God strengthened Elijah to run seventeen miles and then to walk for many days. How can believers tap into God's strength when they are weary?

6. What is the role of God's angels?

7. What did Elijah need to get "renewed for service"?

8. What was God saying to Elijah through the wind, earthquake, fire, and still small voice?

9. What is the responsibility from one generation to the next in fulfilling God's purposes?

10. What mistakes did Elijah make in 1 Kings 19? How did God respond to Elijah and his mistakes?

Chapter Twelve

Ahab, the Slave of Sin
(1 Kings 20:1–22:53)

1. Why did God promise to give Ahab victory over Ben-hadad?

2. What reason was given to Ben-hadad for the Syrian defeat? How did that change his reasoning for the second battle?

3. After his two military victories, how did Ahab fail?

4. What sins did Ahab and Jezebel commit in the matter of Naboth's vineyard?

5. Why did Naboth refuse the king's offer to buy the vineyard? What factors would make it difficult for you to refuse such an offer?

6. How do we see a wife's powerful influence for evil in the relationship of Jezebel and Ahab? How can a wife be an influence for good?

7. What was God's sentence of judgment on the royal couple? What was Ahab's response? What does God's subsequent decision reveal to us about God?

8. In what way was Jehoshaphat a godly leader?

9. What were Jehoshaphat's "three costly compromises"?

10. When Micaiah prophesied truthfully, what great example did he set for us?

Chapter Thirteen

Reflections on Responsibility
(Review)

1. How can one person make a difference? How do we see this in the life of David?

2. Why is it that "success often leads to failure"?

3. How could Solomon be so wise but live a large part of his life in foolishness?

4. Why is it said that national strength and character begin in the home? In what way do you notice this is true in your country?

5. What is the lesson learned from the life of Rehoboam? How can this be made practical in the life of the church?

6. How did Jeroboam waste his opportunity? How instead could he have made the most of it? What opportunities do you currently have? How can you make the most of them?

7. Why is idol worship an insult to both God and people?

8. Why do some leaders tend to abuse their authority? What are Scriptural principles to follow for those with authority in this world?

9. How can believing in God's sovereignty make a difference in our lives?

10. What does this statement mean, "Responsibility means our response to His ability"?